ESSENTIAL STUDY SKILLS

THE COMPLETE GUIDE TO SUCCESS AT UNIVERSITY

Tom Burns and Sandra Sinfield

SAGE Publications
London ● Thousand Oaks ● New Delhi

SAGE Publications Ltd
1 Oliver's Yard
55 City Road
London EC1Y 1SP

SAGE Publications Inc
2455 Teller Road
Thousand Oaks
California 91320

SAGE Publications India Pvt Ltd
B–42 Panchsheel Enclave
PO Box 4109
New Delhi 110 017

British Library Cataloguing in Publication data
A catalogue record for this book is available from the British Library

ISBN-10 0-7619-4957-7   ISBN-13 978-0-7619-4957-2
ISBN-10 0-7619-4958-5 (pbk)   ISBN-13 978-0-7619-4958-9 (pbk)

Library of Congress Control Number: 2002065569

Printed on paper from sustainable sources

Typeset by Pantek Arts Ltd., Maidstone, Kent
Printed and bound in Great Britain by
Cromwell Press Limited, Trowbridge, Wiltshire

CONTENTS

Biographical details

Tom Burns is a Visiting Lecturer at the London Metropolitan University (formerly the University of North London), specialising in study skills programmes and developing resources for foundation to post-graduate level students. He also lectures in media and sociology at Redbridge College, Essex.

Sandra Sinfield is Senior Lecturer and Co-ordinator for Learning and Language Development at the London Metropolitan University (formerly the University of North London). She has developed a range of study skills courses and is also a moderator for access programmes with the London Open College network.

Acknowledgements

The authors would like to thank all the students with whom they have worked – for without their comments, requests, arguments, challenges, feedback and support this book would never have been possible. They would also like to thank Dr James Bentley Philip an exceptional scholar, teacher and friend for his support and encouragement.

A very special thank you to Julius Anthony for his help with the design and the diagrams.

'The effect on our students was like star dust!'
Anne Schofield,
Director of Social Work Studies,
Ruskin College, Oxford, commenting on the authors' teaching.

Introduction

Aims

To help you get the most from this book by giving information on 'how to use this book' and a detailed overview of the rest of the book.

Learning outcomes

That after reading this section and engaging with the activities you will have:

■ gained an overview of the rest of the book

■ considered how to get the most from this book.

Welcome

Welcome to Essential Study Skills! This book is designed to help you become a more effective and happier student. All the activities and suggestions in this book have arisen out of practical work with students in schools, colleges and universities in the United Kingdom over more than 20 years. Students, tutors and course examiners have commented on the effectiveness of the information and activities suggested in this book:
Students: This was the best piece of learning I have ever done!
Examiners: This changes students' lives, not just their study skills.
Tutors: The effect on our students was like stardust.

Each chapter in this book has an overall theme and whilst there might be some slight changes in the presentation of material, certain things will recur throughout the book. Typically there will be a presentation of information – coupled with activities for you to do and questions to answer – followed by commentary and discussion points.

Pens, pencils and paper

We recommend that you work through sections of the book with notepad and pens to hand. Fill in questionnaires and perform many of the activities as you go. Once you have finished a section of the book, reflect on what you have read and done – asking yourself, what does this tell me? How will knowing this make me a more successful student? In this way you will get the most from the book as you go through it – and in the long term.

How to use this book

This is the sort of book that you can work through step by step if you want to – but it has also been designed such that you can dip into different sections of the book as and when you feel they will be useful to you. The trick is to know what *you* want from each section of the book at any particular time.

Activity: How to use this book

Read the Contents of the book:

■ Which sections look useful to you right now? Why is that?

■ Which sections will you look at at a later date?

■ When will you do this reading? Make a note on a calendar.

Now scan the Index pages of the book (these are at the back and they highlight key words that appear throughout the book – and tell you the pages on which they can be found):

■ What words look interesting to you? Make a note – that is, note the topics and note the pages on which they can be found.

■ Have a quick look at some of those pages.

■ What have you discovered?

■ What does this tell you?

Query: Is this the way that you normally approach a book?

Discussion: Reading for academic purposes is usually very different from reading for pleasure. When we read for pleasure many of us read from cover to cover. We enjoy working through the book from beginning to end. We want to know 'what happens next'. We do not rush to the ending for that might spoil our fun.

Reading for study is different to this. Typically we do not ever read a book from cover to cover. We **dip into** books – looking for specific bits of information. We do not need to read the whole book – we might not even need to read a whole chapter…

However, this can feel very uncomfortable. On the one hand we can feel that we are cheating if we do not read the whole book – or we might feel that we will not understand the subject properly – or that we will be missing something.

Sometimes we will have to change the way we normally do things in order to succeed in education.

Reflecting on the first activity

Reflect again: Have another think about the How to use this Book activity – and the discussion points given:

■ Why have we asked you to do the things we have?

■ Why have we told you the above information?

■ What does it all tell you?

Discussion

1 What we have tried to do is to very quickly **demonstrate** to you that there are some successful academic strategies around that help us to study (here it was getting more out of this book). These techniques can help everyone to become a better student; however, they might require us to change some of our behaviours.

2 You might have noticed already that some of these changes are a little uncomfortable. **Change is often uncomfortable** and that can be one reason why sensible and intelligent people sometimes refuse to adopt successful study practices – it just feels too uncomfortable. But the uncomfortable feelings do pass – so when you practise some of the activities suggested in this book be prepared for discomfort – and tell yourself that it will pass.

3 Finally, we have tried to help you become more **in control** of your own learning – to become an active learner. We learn more when we take control of our studies – when we recognise what we want (I'll read that chapter first because…) and when we plan when we will do it (I'll do it on the bus tomorrow on my way to college). All of the advice, strategies, guidelines, tips and tricks in this book are designed to help you become an active learner – an active student. Good luck – and enjoy the book!

Overview of the book – the six steps to success

Overview of the book and a brief introduction to the characteristics of successful study that shape the rest of the book.

■ How to learn and study – with a focus on active learning and joining academic communities.

■ How to organise yourself for study – looking at organisation and time management.

■ How to research and read academically-targeted research and active reading.

■ How to use the overview in your studies (getting the big picture).

■ How to pass exams – memory, learning style, revision and exam techniques (big picture – small steps).

■ How to learn creatively – in your notemaking and when approaching assignments.

■ How to build your confidence – in the academic environment.

■ How to succeed in group work.

■ How to prepare better assignments – by understanding assessment, communication and the 'what, why and how' of essays, reports, presentations and seminars.

■ How to be reflective – that is, how to reflect on your learning so that you make the learning conscious and so that you become aware of your own learning strategies.

And students have said:

'This really sets students up to succeed!'

'It opened up different strategies, learning strategies, … and now I don't feel inferior.'

'And you go, **yes**, and it really spurs you on!'

Starting to study at university or college or returning to a higher level of study, especially after a break, can make you feel anxious: how will you cope with it all? How will you manage the notemaking, organising your time, the assessments – essays, reports, presentations, exams! Everyone else looks as though they know what's going on and you are the only one who looks, sounds and feels like a fool! Everybody else is a good student – and no one has the same fears and worries as you! What can you do?

Our work with students, examiners and tutors has told us that there are certain study and academic skills and practices that, if learned and rehearsed, can help us all to be better students – and to be happier and more successful when studying. We have based this book on the following propositions, and we have called these the **six steps to study success**. We are going to introduce them quickly here – and then develop them in much more detail throughout the rest of this book.

Remember, just because these ideas are in a list does not mean that the first thing mentioned is more important than the last – they are all equally important and they must all be engaged with every time we study (or tackle any other task) if we want to do well.

The six step propositions

■ Good students are made, not born.

■ Everybody needs the big picture (or overview).

■ Creativity is essential – and it can be developed.

■ Understanding the 'what, why and how' of assessment is vital.

■ Dealing with your emotions is crucial.

■ Without reflection there is no learning.

We have devised a mnemonic to help you remember these six steps – SOCCER:

S – Study techniques and practices

O – Overview

C – Creativity

C – Communicate effectively

E – Emotions

R – Review, review, review.

Good students are made, not born

It is all too easy to think that we are not 'cut out' for studying. Often negative experiences at school can lead many people to believe that studying is not for them – they are just not good students. Our work with students of all ages and 'abilities' leads us to believe that most of us can learn to become good students – what gets in the way is the belief that it should all come naturally.

Why should you think that you 'ought' to know how to study effectively? If you wanted to be a fire fighter or a farmer or a chef or a carpenter you would know that you would have to learn how to be one. You would guess that you could also learn certain tricks of the trade that would make the job easier or more effective. If we think of studying like this it can become easier. All the way through this book we will look at the constituent study and academic skills that can help you to succeed – with a special focus on organising yourself for study in Chapter 2.

Everybody needs the big picture (or overview)

Whilst it is true that we tend to learn things in pieces, one step at a time, this process is helped if we know what we are learning and how the subject area will be covered (the syllabus or timetable). To use a simple analogy, it is like a jigsaw puzzle – it is much easier to put the pieces together if we have the picture on the box to guide us.

Programmes of study – from GCSE to university courses – have all been designed to have an overall shape and structure. It helps us as students to make sense of the whole course – each lecture and each piece of reading – if we understand that overall structure – if we have the big picture – before we start. Typically this will involve learning how to make the best of course *aims* and *outcomes* (see particularly Chapter 4).

Creativity is essential – and it can be developed

There is a lot of 'common sense' about being a successful student – and we don't want to criticise common sense. But if you want to do that little bit more, if you want studying to be a little bit easier or more interesting – then a touch of creativity is needed.

If you give back to lecturers what they have told you – if you just use their examples and read the books that they recommend – then you will be a strong, average student. To get a little further you have to be creative – but how can you do that? We look at brainstorming, question matrixing and, most importantly, pattern notemaking (see Chapter 6). These are techniques that in their various ways encourage a different or more original approach to your studies.

Understanding the 'what, why and how' of assessment is vital

Just as we cannot just 'know' how to study, we cannot 'know' what an essay, report or presentation is. These things have specific shapes to them (what), they have specific learning and assessment purposes (why) and there are tried and tested ways of approaching them that can be developed (how). In order to help you develop successful assessment techniques, we devote a whole, long chapter (9) on exploring the essay, report, presentation and seminar.

Dealing with your emotions is crucial

Studying and learning may be cognitive or intellectual activities, but for most of us they are fraught with emotion also. If we do not tackle our own emotional responses to the different things that we encounter as students – we will never be able to benefit from our positive responses or overcome our negative ones.

In Chapter 7 we explore the roles of fear and self-confidence in the academic environment. In Chapter 8 we look at how to approach group work positively.

Without reflection there is no learning

There is much evidence around to suggest that learning involves an active selection of what to learn – and how to learn it. Throughout the book we will be examining different revision/review strategies, and in the last chapter we will pull all this together with a detailed look at the reflective learning diary and a detailed review of the whole book itself. In the process you will be encouraged to explore not only what you have learned but how you learned it.

How to approach each chapter

1 Before you read, set your own goals – know why you are reading a section of this book. Know what you want to get from it.

2 Whilst reading keep asking questions – what is going on here? What does this tell me? Why are they telling me that? How will knowing this help me?

3 After reading, take the time to reflect on what you have read – and make a few notes to make your learning conscious.

● **Tip:** Have a look at the first part of Chapter 3.

Review points

By reading this introductory chapter – and engaging with the activities set – you should now have:

- ☐ a detailed overview of the rest of the book

- ☐ an understanding of how to approach the book such that you get the most from it

- ☐ an awareness that developing your potential as a student will involve you in change

- ☐ an awareness of the six steps to success – the propositions that shape and inform the rest of the book itself.

How to learn and study

Aims

To prepare you for academic study by examining learning and studying, and by exploring the nature of academic communities.

Learning outcomes

That after reading through this chapter, and engaging with the activities, you will have:

■ considered the processes of learning

■ realised the active nature of learning

■ explored aspects of academic study

■ gained an understanding of academic communities

■ considered the sorts of activities that go on in universities and colleges

■ engaged with various activities that have reinforced your understanding of the different parts of the chapter.

Introduction

In the previous section we argued that no one is born just knowing how to learn and how to study. In this chapter we are going to consider the nature of learning and studying – we will move on to explore what it means to join an academic community, especially the various communities of the university. We will cover how teaching and learning is organised in universities and we will close with very specific advice on places to go, people to meet and things to do in your university.

What is learning?

Whilst there are various definitions of learning we are going to explore one that is associated with study skills. This definition can be used to make the link between skills and learning.

Devine (1987) argues that learning is not one thing but a series of activities:

- gathering new ideas and information

- recording them

- organising them

- making sense of them

- remembering them

- using them.

We are going to examine these in more detail here.

Active learning

First let us look at the list itself again. Does anything strike you about this list? One thing that we notice is that there are a lot of verbs. Learning is doing – it is active – it is not just storing bits of information in the brain ready to spill them out onto an exam paper and then forgetting them! Everything covered in the rest of this book will build your active learning skills: we will encourage you to engage with, question and understand your course work and to express yourself successfully within the academic conventions of your subjects. Let us now look at that list in some detail.

Gather

Learning is about gathering new ideas and information. We call this research and it can involve taking information in from classes, lectures, seminars, tutorials, discussion, practicals, reading (texts, journals, newspapers and more), watching films, videos and television programmes.

Record

Then you have to record, organise and make sense of that information. Recording typically involves some form of notemaking activity. That is, recording points that you have heard, read or seen, in some form or other so that you have a record of them. You will go back to your notes at some point in order to use the information that you have recorded.

Organise

When we research we encounter information in many forms, in many places and at different times. What we are doing here is encountering the various accepted and contested knowledge-claims for our subject (see Len Holmes (2002) e-mail in Chapter 10). What we have to do is rearrange the information to make sense of it for ourselves. In the process we have to notice that one piece of information might contradict something else that we have already encountered – and that other things that we discover agree with or 'back up' each other.

Make sense of

So we have to look for information in a variety of places – then we have to rearrange and record it for ourselves. During this process we have to notice that certain ideas agree with, whilst others contradict, each other. Basically, we have to think about all the different things that we have heard, read or seen and make sense of them for ourselves. We have to understand it.

When looking at this aspect of studying, people often talk about **surface** and **deep** learning. Surface is where you might record key bits of information – names and dates of battles, for example. Deep is where you understand the significance of the events that occurred – this battle was actually the turning point in the war and brought about... Or that bit of evidence contradicts what I read in ...

That is why we encourage an active learning approach – an approach that gets you continually asking questions of and doing things with the information that you acquire. An active learning style is designed to move you from surface to deep learning – and it also helps you to remember those important names, dates and events – because they are useful too!

● **Tip:** Good notemaking skills can help you to organise and understand information as you gather and record it – see Chapter 6 How to learn creatively.

Remember it

So we have looked at acquiring information as actively as possible, but this information is not yours unless you remember it.

As you listen to or read material in your subject area, you have to select important information and then make a conscious decision to remember it. In terms of being a successful student, we can call this ability revision and exam technique – and it is covered in Chapter 5 How to pass exams (big picture – small steps).

But a quick word on this now. Do not try to remember everything you need to know just before your exams. This does not work – and it does not help you remember information 'for keeps', for life.

● **Tip:** Learning or remembering information starts at the beginning of a course.

Use it

Finally you have to be able to use the information yourself for it to be really yours. You have to be able to communicate what you know – be able to explain or write about it, to discuss it with other people – and we have to undertake that communication in the way that our subject wants us to (see Chapter 9).

I don't like to be tested!

The problem perhaps with communicating what we know as students is that it usually happens as an assessment: so we do not feel that we are communicating – we feel that we are being tested! Typically no one likes to be tested – it means that we can fail – we might show ourselves up. These thoughts bring negative feelings and these negative feelings, whilst being completely natural in the circumstances, do not help us get the most out of communicating.

When we communicate what we know, we do not pour out ready formed and already polished words – what we actually do is struggle to form our ideas. This struggle, in speaking or writing, is actually a really important part of the learning process.

Therefore, the argument that we will follow through in Chapter 9 is that the beauty of communicating what you know is that it also helps you to understand and learn the material.

I already do that

This is something that you most probably know already, for example, have you noticed how you understand a topic better once you have discussed it with someone? This is because, when you discuss a new topic with someone, your brain works on the information – and you make it your own. It is exactly the same when we struggle to write about something.

Conclusion

Hopefully we have encouraged you to think of learning slightly differently from how you might have thought about it before. We have tried to encourage you to see that learning is an activity – or series of activities – and that you have to be an active learner in order to learn anything. There now follow some activities that will help you think about your learning.

Activity: Good and bad learning

Before we finish this section, we'd now like you to think back to your own past learning experiences. In particular, think about the conditions that help you to learn – and the things that might get in the way of your learning. Make brief notes to answer the questions below:

1 Think back to a previous successful learning experience. It does not have to have been at school – it could be learning to drive or sky dive. Now try to work out why it was successful – why did you learn?

2 Now think back to an unsuccessful learning experience. What was it? Why did little or no learning take place?

3 Looking over these good and bad experiences of yours – can you sum up 'things that help learning to happen' and 'things that prevent learning'? Make a list.

4 If you wish, use your list to write two paragraphs: one on 'Things that help me learn' and one on 'Things that stop me learning'.

5 Once you have completed your own thoughts, compare your paragraphs with those given by another student, below:

   – Things that helped me to learn were an interesting course with a good teacher – you know, one that had enthusiasm for the subject and lots of energy. It also helped that I knew why I wanted to do that course, I had chosen it for myself and I actually wanted to learn. I was committed – I'd turn up and do the work – because I wanted do. Not only that but there was a really supportive atmosphere – I felt challenged and stretched – but it was also safe to make mistakes… Nobody laughed at you or made you feel a fool.

   – The worst thing I ever did was at school. I had to do the course – it was compulsory – but I never really saw the point of it. Not only that, the teacher was a bit of a bully and humiliated people when they got things wrong. Also I just felt so powerless all the time – we never knew what we were doing or why or when or how. It was a nightmare and one of the reasons that I left school the minute I could!

Discussion: Were these points like your own? What does this tell us? One thing could be that if we are going to be successful when learning, then we must **want** to learn – we must be interested and motivated and we should have our own clear goals. On the other hand, what seems to stop people from learning is feeling unmotivated, confused, unhappy and powerless.

Now look at your points again – how can you make use of this information to help yourself be a better learner and a better student? Things to ask yourself:

■ How do I learn best?

■ What subjects do I enjoy?

■ What job do I want later on?

■ What sorts of courses will help me get where I want to go?

● **Tip:** Whenever you start to study anything – from a long course (like a three or four year degree programme) to a short unit of a course (a 15 week module) – sit down and set your own personal goals for that course. Write your goals on stickers and put them over your desk. There are no right or wrong reasons – the trick is to know **your** reasons – and to use this information to keep you motivated and interested when doing your studying.

Things that other students have said are their reasons for studying:

– I want to know more about this subject

– I want a better career

– I want to earn more money

– I want to make new friends...

Activity: The learning contract

We have recommended that you always set your own goals when studying. In this activity we are going to take that a step further and consider using **learning contracts** as motivational tools. A learning contract is where you work out for yourself:

■ your reasons for doing something

■ what you are prepared to do to realise your own goals

■ what might stop you – and

■ what is 'in it' for you – what you actually get out of it at the end or how it will benefit your life in some way.

Activity: Essential Study Skills: The learning contract

Why not write a learning contract for this book. Think about the following questions and try to come up with some answers:

1 Why am I reading this book?
2 What am I prepared to do to get the most from this book?
3 What might stop me?
4 What's in it for me?

When you have drawn up your learning contract stick it on the wall. When you settle down to read another bit of this book, look at the contract and remind yourself of your own goals. (For an example of a learning contract see Figure 1.1.)

Discussion:
Your learning contract for this book could help you get more from a particular bit of reading. When you don't feel like doing any reading – but feel that you 'should' – look at the contract and see if that gives you the motivation to proceed.

● **Tip: Always** do your own learning contract for any course that you do – use it whenever you need to push yourself a bit to get the work done!

What is studying?

Much of the learning that we do as human beings does not actually come in the form of studying. We learn how to cook perhaps by watching other people or trying out recipes from a book. Hopefully, we do not expect to get things right first go: we expect to learn through trial and error, we are prepared to practise until we have got the hang of cooking – especially when we tackle new recipes. Studying can **feel** very different from this!

Study

Studying and learning can be the same thing – though sometimes they are not. But when we talk about studying we tend to be referring to the way that teaching and learning is organised in formal programmes of study. We also talk about the work that we have to do as students to benefit from those programmes of study – and to pass the courses that we take. This book explores 'study' and 'studying' with a special focus on the study and academic skills and practices necessary for success in the university system, but the advice applies to all learning situations.

Before we go on to explore what happens in university and what it can mean to become a student, the following questionnaire explores how you **feel** about yourself as a student.

Activity: Personal skills review: focusing questionnaire

1 How do you feel about yourself as a student at the moment?

2 What study techniques do you use at the moment? How successful are these? Which do you want to improve?

3 How positive do you feel about being a student? How committed are you to developing your skills? What are you prepared to do to improve? How much time and energy are you prepared to put in?

4 How organised are you? (If you have brought up a family or juggled work with a hobby or family, then you are used to organising your life. This is a useful, transferable skill.) If you have studied before, did you have set times to work? Do you have a place to study? What do you need here?

5 What reading do you do at the moment? Are you happy with your reading skills? What do you need here?

6 Do you use your local library? Do you know anything about libraries?

7 Do you make notes when you study? Are you happy with your notes? What do you do with your notes? What do you need here?

8 What sorts of writing do you do at the moment (e.g. letters to friends, business correspondence etc.)? Have you written essays before? What sort of marks did you get? Are you happy with that? What do you want here?

9 Have you ever had to make a presentation to a group of people? (A presentation is a talk of a set length to a specific audience, usually on a specific topic.) How did it go? What do you feel about the idea of having to do presentations on your course? What do you want to know about presentations?

10 Have you revised for and sat exams? How did it go? How do you feel about your memory? How do you feel about exams? What do you need to know about revision and exam techniques?

Discussion: This list breaks down academic practices into some necessary constituent elements – you cannot write an essay, for example, if you cannot organise your time, make useful notes or read academic texts successfully. The rest of this book will take you through these constituent activities so that you not only understand their significance but you also get the opportunity to practise and reflect upon them.

● **Tip:** Your answers to these questions will tell you what you want to get from each section of this book. Use them!

Now look back at your learning contract for this book. Can you add things to it in the light of your answers to the questionnaire? If so – do so. (And don't worry that you did not get your contract 'right' first go! Learning is not about being right all the time. It is about building up your information. Adding to it when you can.)

Once you have completed the **personal skills review** – and amended your learning contract you should really be in a position to get the most from your reading of this book. We have another preliminary activity for

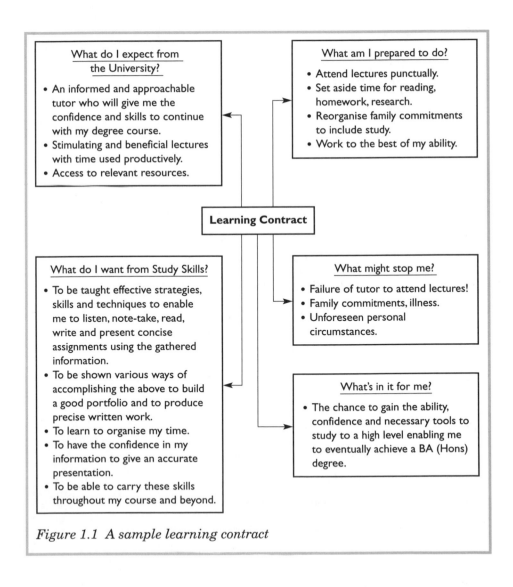

What do I expect from the University?

- An informed and approachable tutor who will give me the confidence and skills to continue with my degree course.
- Stimulating and beneficial lectures with time used productively.
- Access to relevant resources.

What am I prepared to do?

- Attend lectures punctually.
- Set aside time for reading, homework, research.
- Reorganise family commitments to include study.
- Work to the best of my ability.

Learning Contract

What do I want from Study Skills?

- To be taught effective strategies, skills and techniques to enable me to listen, note-take, read, write and present concise assignments using the gathered information.
- To be shown various ways of accomplishing the above to build a good portfolio and to produce precise written work.
- To learn to organise my time.
- To have the confidence in my information to give an accurate presentation.
- To be able to carry these skills throughout my course and beyond.

What might stop me?

- Failure of tutor to attend lectures!
- Family commitments, illness.
- Unforeseen personal circumstances.

What's in it for me?

- The chance to gain the ability, confidence and necessary tools to study to a high level enabling me to eventually achieve a BA (Hons) degree.

Figure 1.1 A sample learning contract

you to do – and this is also designed to get you thinking about some of your feelings with respect to study and being a student. So, have a look at our **hopes and fears statements** – fill in some responses to the statements and then compare your responses to some given by other students, below.

Activity: Hopes and fears statements

We have gathered together some of the things that we have heard new students say. Have a look at these statements and jot down your own responses to them.

1 I'm not sure that I'll find enough time to study.

2 I'm apprehensive that my studies will affect the rest of my life.

3 I find it hard to concentrate for long periods.

4 I'm really looking forward to the challenge of studying again.

5 I haven't written an essay for ages and I'm anxious about putting pen to paper.

6 I was never good at school in the first place – how will I cope with this?

7 My memory isn't as good as it used to be.

8 I'm worried that the work will be difficult and I won't be able to understand it.

9 I enjoy working with other people – and discussing things.

10 I'm worried because English isn't my first language.

11 I'll find it hard to get down to work.

12 I'm not sure how my friends and family will react to my studies.

13 I'm good at organising my time.

14 I'm worried that I'll find it hard to cope with the difficult reading. I wish I could read faster.

15 I bet everyone on the course will be more used to studying than I am.

16 I'm not sure how to cope with the distractions at home.

17 I'm afraid that I'll fall behind with my work.

18 I'm glad that I have somewhere quiet to study.

19 I'm not sure how much to discuss my work with other people. Isn't that cheating?

20 Deadlines give me the energy to do things.

21 I get a real sense of achievement out of finishing things.

▶

22 I'm not very good at spelling.

23 I'm never sure when to use a comma or a full stop.

24 I've forgotten all the rules of grammar.

25 I can write letters but I don't know the sort of language you have to know to write essays.

26 I know what to say but I can't find the right words.

27 I don't have a wide enough vocabulary.

28 I have plenty of ideas but I don't seem able to put them together.

29 I'm all right once I get started, but I have a block about starting.

30 I just don't know how to set about writing an essay.

Discussion: Phew! That was a long list! How do you feel now? Here are a couple of things that might have happened:

■ just writing your fears down or saying them out loud made you see that they are not so bad after all

■ seeing a list like this was reassuring – you are not alone!

Did either of these things happen for you? Why don't you try to find someone to discuss your list with? If you can find someone – move on to the **Talking it over** activity.

Activity: Talking it over

Find someone to talk to about your responses – preferably a study partner or colleague, someone who is also studying with you. A partner can make all the difference when studying. A partner can help break down some of your fears. A partner can share the study load. And of course a partner gives many opportunities for active learning – for you can talk about and discuss things all the time. Here it would help if you chose someone who has completed his or her own list.

With your partner:

1 Look at the similarities and differences between your lists.

2 Consider whether any of the statements that express anxiety really matter.

3 Can you think of any solutions that are relevant to this stage of your work?

Discussion: Has your discussion with your study partner helped at all? Why don't you now look at some responses collected from other students?

Hopes and fears statements and responses:

▦ *I'm not sure that I'll find enough time to study.*
Well I guess that's why there's a question about organisation and being able to juggle our time. I also notice that there is a section later on about organisation and time management.

▦ *I'm apprehensive that my studies will affect the rest of my life.*
Well, being a student is going to have a dramatic impact on my life, I can see that. I will not have as much time for friends and family – nor to do the other things that I really like doing perhaps. But there again, life does change; it's about changes and changing. And as it has already mentioned here, change can be very uncomfortable – and becoming a student just makes you realise this a bit more!

▦ *I find it hard to concentrate for long periods.*
I shall start by concentrating for short periods and try to build up to longer study periods. I don't have to get it all right straight away.

▦ *I'm really looking forward to the challenge of studying again.*
So am I! It makes me feel good about me.

▦ *I haven't written an essay for ages and I'm anxious about putting pen to paper.*
But that's why I'm using this book.

▦ *I was never good at school in the first place – how will I cope with this?*
I know what you mean – but I didn't like school, maybe that's why I didn't do well there. It's different now.

▦ *My memory isn't as good as it used to be.*
I've heard that this isn't really true. What happens when we get older is that we pay more attention to what we forget – we should notice what we are getting right more. Also, when it comes to studying, I have never realised before how much effort I will have to put in to remembering things. I thought that the brain just remembered stuff or it did not. I can see now that I have to choose what to remember and how to remember it. It's different – but I hope that I can learn to do that!

▦ *I'm worried that the work will be difficult and I won't be able to understand it.*
I noticed the point about 'trial and error' – I am going to try to be brave and be prepared to learn from my mistakes. I'm also going to ask questions if I don't understand! And I've bought an English dictionary and a Subject dictionary to help me cope with the language of my subject!

▦ *I enjoy working with other people – and discussing things.*
I'm going to have to find a study partner because I really do like talking things over – I've done some of my best learning in the canteen once class is over.

▶

■ *I'm worried because English isn't my first language.*
My daughter is better at English than I am and she has said that she will help me. She also thinks that I'm being very brave studying in English – which makes me feel strong instead of foolish!

■ *I'll find it hard to get down to work.*
It is hard to study – for everybody. I have a special place to sit, and when I am there I 'feel' like a student. Sometimes I trick myself into sitting there – I say, just sit there for five minutes and see what happens – before I know it I have started to work and it is alright after all.

■ *I'm not sure how my friends and family will react to my studies.*
Yes – this can be a problem. I do know people who have a really hard time: their friends think they'll become snobs or their children start to play up every time they try to get some work done… I guess if we want them to understand what we are doing – and support us – we have to explain what we are doing and build some time for them into our study timetable!

■ *I'm good at organising my time.*
I find I have two approaches: one is to be very organised – I make lists of all the things that I have to do and I work through them. The other system is I sit down amongst a pile of work and plunge in and just get on with it. Both systems seem to work sometimes. This tells me there is no one right way to do anything – but that I do have to keep on top of things or else everything feels worse!

■ *I'm worried that I'll find it hard to cope with the difficult reading. I wish I could read faster.*
I've heard that academic reading does get easier with practice – I certainly hope so. Still I suppose it's got to take up some time – it's not a detective story is it?

■ *I bet everyone on the course will be more used to studying than I am.*
I also bet that I'm the only one who's frightened and I'm the only one whose family doesn't understand them… It's not true really, is it?

■ *I'm not sure how to cope with the distractions at home.*
Well, I've got a friend who works from home, so I know it can be done. She puts the answerphone on; she does not open the door – and things like that. The problem arises when we actually **want** to be distracted because that is easier than doing the work!

■ *I'm afraid that I'll fall behind with my work.*
I'm hoping the section on organising my time will help me with that!

■ *I'm glad that I have somewhere quiet to study.*
Lucky you – I don't! Anyway, I've heard that this is another case where there is no one right way of working. Some people work best in the quiet, others like noise …

▶

■ *I'm not sure how much to discuss my work with other people. Isn't that cheating?*
I know the answer to this one. Talking isn't cheating, it's active learning. I like the sound of that.

■ *Deadlines give me the energy to do things.*
Without deadlines I do find it difficult to finish things. At the same time I know that I mustn't leave it all till the last minute – I must pace myself through an assignment.

■ *I get a real sense of achievement out of finishing things.*
I love it when I hand a piece of work in on time. But I do know other people who hate finishing things off. They just keep on reading and reading. I guess that sometimes it's difficult to know when you've done enough work.

■ *I'm not very good at spelling.*
I'm going to use the spell checker on my computer. I've also heard that it is a good idea to build up your own dictionary of difficult words. I've already bought a small exercise book to do this.

■ *I'm never sure when to use a comma or a full stop.*

■ *I've forgotten all the rules of grammar.*
Punctuation was not my strong point either. My trick is to write in relatively short sentences. This keeps my meaning clear. When it comes to using the new words that I am learning on my course – well, I use them when it is easier to do that than to try and explain what I am talking about without using that word. Like everything else, I hope it gets easier with practice.

■ *I can write letters but I don't know the sort of language you have to know to write essays.*
I think I'll try to do what that other person says – get the exercise book to jot down the new words and use them when I understand them and if it makes sense to do so.

■ *I know what to say but I can't find the right words.*
I will try the little exercise book tip, too. I do know that it's not about talking as if you have swallowed a dictionary – it's about expressing yourself effectively. This usually means writing simply and clearly.

■ *I don't have a wide enough vocabulary.*
A friend of mine coped with this by writing new words on Post-its and sticking them up all over his flat. He said he got to learn them really quickly that way.

■ *I have plenty of ideas but I don't seem able to put them together.*
Apparently planning helps us get our ideas together – and that's covered in here somewhere.

▶

■ *I'm all right once I get started, but I have a block about starting.*
Yes – that is why sometimes you do have to trick yourself into starting, you know, I'll just give it five minutes… and see if that helps.

■ *I just don't know how to set about writing an essay.*
Again, I don't think that I have to know about this just yet. If I worry about too many things at once, then I get nothing done at all.

Query: How do you feel now? Hopefully you have found it useful to cover these things. Remember there is often no right or wrong way to approach being a student – as long as you want to do well – and you are prepared to put some effort in – you should discover your own way of doing well.

By now you should have a sense of what the rest of the book has to offer you in terms of building your study and academic skills and practices. By filling in a learning contract, you should also have set clear goals with respect to what you hope to get from reading the book. And you should also know 'what is in it for you'. We are now going to look at universities in some detail. Before you read on, remember – be that active, questioning student we recommended above. So:

■ Ask yourself why such a section is in this book?

■ Think briefly – what do you already know on the subject?

■ What do you want to find out?

■ How will knowing those things make you a better student?

Studying and university

Deciding to go to university is a big decision for anyone – in this section we are going to explore the different universities that you can attend, with a quick look at just who goes to university these days. We will move on to consider what it means to go to university, with a special emphasis on joining academic communities. Finally we shall give advice on how to get the most out of your time at university by exploring the different 'sources of information' that are available to you there – and by listing the various things to do and people to see in your university.

Which university?

If you are not yet at university, you might be thinking about which one to go to. Higher Education teaching and learning in England typically takes place in what we tend to call 'old' and 'new' universities. Some courses do take place in Higher Education Institutes, but here we shall briefly be discussing both the old and new universities.

Old universities

The old universities range from the well-known and traditional such as Oxford and Cambridge to institutions such as York and Derby to the modern campuses of East Anglia and Essex. These universities are primarily research-based institutions. Tutors there have a focus on personal research with the expectation that their research would take knowledge and understanding of that area forward. Typically this would make them leaders in their particular fields.

Students choose to attend these universities to receive instruction from research-based tutors – from the recognised subject 'leaders'. At the same time, they become part of the wider community of a high status university. This means that when their degree programme is over, they still have a relationship with a highly respected institution.

The idea is that students form networks with the other students – and even with the tutors at the university. These networks help students to pass on information and to find employment.

This is one reason why Microsoft went to Cambridge: they wanted to plug into the research networks that exist at Cambridge – and also to be able to access the whole student body and networks that would come out of that university.

New universities

The new universities generally sprang from the old polytechnics. The polytechnic idea was to take higher education to the broader mass of people – those often excluded from or not encouraged into the old universities. Polytechnics often taught more vocational (job orientated) degree programmes and, typically, their emphasis was more on successful teaching strategies rather than on research *per se*. That is, polytechnics, such as those of North and East London, wanted to reach out to the wider communities at their doors and offer them supportive teaching and learning environments.

In 1992 the Government opened up the university charter so that the old polytechnics could lobby to become universities. The new universities, whilst they were expected to develop their research base, were tacitly also expected to keep a 'widening participation' brief, and still reach out to what has been called the 'non-traditional' student.

Who goes to university?

In the old days, and right up to very recently, only five per cent of the English population went to university. This is a very small proportion of the population of the whole country. Critics of this system argued that the education system in England was geared up not to educate but to prevent people from getting up the education ladder. The old O levels, they argued, were designed to stop people from doing A levels; and A levels in their turn were designed to stop people from going to university. (This is one of those 'contested' claims, that is, not everybody would agree with this analysis of the situation.)

This was exacerbated by a classical degree structure that did not encourage flexibility and choice. For example, if you wanted to study English Literature at degree level, you would have needed O levels in French and Latin and possibly in classical Greek also. Many of these subjects were not even taught in state secondary schools.

This system meant that degree programmes were taken up by people who already had an understanding of the degree system – perhaps because their families all had degrees. These people would be groomed to make the right choices at 13 to get them onto the degree programmes of their choice. They would definitely be in secondary schools that would prepare them for the university of their choice – the university that would help them form lifelong networks to advance their careers.

All change

There have been changes to university recruitment recently and it is now expected that upwards of 50% of 18 year olds will be attending university in England in the future.

This book is designed to make university study easier for everybody – but it might be especially useful for you if you are the first in your family to go to university, if you are unsure of exactly what it means to be a student – and if you are slightly unsure of what to do at university, why to do it, and when!

So what university should I choose?

Basically everyone should consider his or her own reasons for actually going to university in the first place. What is it for you: convenience, money or fun? Many students these days choose the university closest to home – this is either convenient, because you do not have to move, or economic, because you do not have to feed yourself, your parents will do that. The fun reason might be that you have heard that Manchester, say, has a good nightlife – so Manchester University seems like a good idea!

These may not seem like world shattering reasons to go to university, but they are the reasons that real students give, and they illustrate a point. You have to choose your university by thinking about why **you** are going to university in the first place. So what about you:

- Do you want to study at a high status institution that will plug you into a high powered network of contacts?

- Or are you going to study a subject because of personal interest?

- Are you studying in the hope of getting a better job?

- Do you want to plug into up-to-the-minute research?

- Or are you more interested in finding a university with an emphasis on supportive teaching?

Maybe none of these things seems important to you – but you have found a very interesting course somewhere and you would just like to do that? Well, that's fine, too.

And the winner is?

Remember though when making your choice, **all** universities do have subject specialisms. Whilst Cambridge might give us our television entertainers, every university these days builds links with particular industries – small or large, local or national, private or public. They will also link with NGOs (non-government organisations) such as charities. The trick is to find out what is going on at which institution. Then choose the university that is the best: for the subject that you have chosen to do, or the area in which you want to work – or the best nightlife …

● **Tip:** Use university websites to search for information. Note what post-graduate courses they offer – this will indicate the university's specialist subjects.

Throughout this book we try to stress that there are no rigid right or wrong choices for many of these things. There is only *your* set of reasons – and *your* choices. But whatever your reasons for going to university – and whichever university you eventually do choose – you will have to work at making it a successful venture for yourself. If you are already at university, it is not too late to start making even more of your time there.

We can all network

If you do want to make contacts at university that could help you throughout your working life, you will have to make the effort to meet the people who will make this happen for you. This means that as well as checking out the subject specialisms and post-graduate opportunities at your university, you will need to notice what **work placements** are possible and which **societies** and **organisations** exist at your university. Then you will need to make time to join them.

Even if the thought of making contacts in this way does not appeal to you, it would still be a good idea to have a look at the clubs and societies at your university. For example, if you wanted to be a DJ, it would be good to join the Entertainment Society. You could then have the opportunity to get involved in booking acts for the Student Union, you can move on to creating your own DJing opportunities. If you wanted to work in television, join the television society – and so on. If the society you want does not exist – start it! Make something happen!

You know it makes sense

Universities are changing:

- Five per cent of the population used to go to university.

- Fifty per cent of 18 year olds are expected to go to university.

- There has been a rise in mature students at some universities.

- Some universities have many overseas students.

All these things represent change – and **opportunity**! Remember, whatever the makeup of the student population at your university, this is going to be the percentage that will earn more, live longer and be healthier. Being a student does open doors for you – and it allows you to meet people and make contacts that you could not make in any other way. Grab the opportunity.

Joining academic communities

Of course university is more than just joining societies and going to the best nightclubs. You will also be joining an academic institution. So, whatever your previous opinions about yourself – jock, ladette, housewife and mother, wage slave, entrepreneur – it is now time to see yourself as an academic.

When you go to university, whether you are aware of it or not, you are joining an academic community. Often you are actually joining several academic communities. These might be the community of:

- the whole university

- your department or faculty

- your school (your subject)

- your module/course choices.

As with other communities, academic communities have ground rules, traditions and a sense of self. These will inform and influence the ways that you are expected to behave as a student generally – but more importantly as a student of a particular subject. History, Business, Pharmacology, Computing – all the subjects that you can study all have specific academic practices, that is particular ways of being researched and of being studied and understood. As well as knowing how to learn and how to study generally, you will need to know how to study your subject: that is, you will have to become familiar with the academic practices of your subject.

Epistemology

Knowledge of academic practices is sometimes called developing your academic literacy or developing an awareness of the **epistemology**, or theory of knowledge, of the subject and typically this means knowing the 'what, why and how' of your subject. That is, you must know what counts as argument and evidence in your subject. By argument we do not mean the everyday use of the term – to disagree or fight – we are talking about how propositions are put together: how one gets to say that something is 'so' in your subject. This will also mean that you will have to make an effort to learn how to communicate in your subject.

The communication strategies – and the epistemology – will be slightly different depending on whether you are a biologist or an historian, a student of film or English literature. But one basic principle will be the same for all subjects: you must develop an understanding of what has gone before (the existing literature) before you will be expected to move on. And moving on will involve building on what has gone before.

The first year is an introductory year

Hence the first year of most degree programmes is designed to lay a good foundation in your subject by introducing you to the existing literature – thus helping you get to grips with the epistemology of your subject. Often, you will not be told that this is what is happening – but it is what is happening. So in the first year you will be introduced to the theories, the people, the dates that have traditionally held significance in your subject. Notice these! You will be building on them throughout your time as a student of that subject – and beyond.

In the first year you will be expected to learn how to 'argue' in the way that you have to in your subject. This means that this is the year where you will have to learn to use argument and evidence like an historian or a biologist, like a philosopher or an educationalist. You will have to notice the rules of your subject – and you will be expected to follow those rules.

Make an impact

Further, although the first year, as a foundation year, will generally not count towards the class (level) of your degree, it is the year when many of your tutors will be meeting you for the first time and making up their minds as to what sort of student you are. So do not treat the first year as a throw away, casual year. This is the year when you start to make the tutors notice you.

On the whole, tutors will be hoping for – and noticing – students who are interested in the subject, who are motivated and who are prepared to think. They will want to see that you contribute to class discussion and that you put effort into tasks. The opinion they form of you in the first year may have a big impact on your later success.

If a tutor begins to see you as a good student, they will treat you as one. They will see your work as the work of a good student. Conversely if you come across as a casual student, not really interested in the subject and not prepared to make an effort, this may well be how they receive and mark your work.

So the first year is the year to definitely start seeing yourself as an academic – even if you are the first person in your family to have gone to university. And as you gain the foundation to your subject and lay the foundations of yourself as a student, be interested and do think – and learn how to communicate that in the right way.

And remember, the things that you are interested in at university will most probably be the threads that you follow as you take up a career and work in the related industries or services afterwards. You will do better at both university and work if you choose a subject that you enjoy and that does actually interest you.

Teaching, learning and sources of information

As we have mentioned above, when we come to university we join academic communities that have established ways of teaching and learning already in place. It is very important for you to understand the various teaching and learning systems so that you can make the most of the opportunities they offer you. Here we are going to explore the most common teaching and learning systems, and at the same time we will give you some things to think about as you go.

The lecture

Usually this involves one lecturer plus a large group of students – this can be 150 or more. The lecturer is an expert, often a researcher at the cutting edge of the subject. A lecture is supposed to seed independent research, and thus acts as a starting point – not an end point – for student thought and understanding. The lecturer speaks – students should listen and note down key points. The purpose of the lecture is to give a shortcut to information – though never 'all you need to know' on the subject. Further, students get to hear the language of their subject being used – thus this models argument and evidence for that subject. Sometimes the lecturer is alive enough to answer questions, so make sure that you do ask useful questions when the opportunity arises.

● **Tip:** Always prepare before you attend a lecture. Think – what is it about? Why are they giving it? How will it help you gain an understanding of the subject? How will it help you with your assignment?

Seminar

Typically a lecturer (or a research student) plus 10-30 students. The name comes from semen or seed. The seminar (and tutorial) system has developed from the Platonic idea that students can be led towards learning by informed discussion with a sage (wise person). Thus the idea is that student thinking is encouraged through tutor-led discussion. A seminar is often linked to a lecture programme and the seminar is designed to extend or deepen the knowledge of the area previously covered in the associated lecture.

Students may be asked to lead seminars of their own (see Chapter 9) or to prepare for seminars in specific ways: for example by reading a particular article or chapter prior to attending the seminar. Be warned – you are expected to participate in discussion and to benefit from that discussion. Be ready to talk and to listen to what is going on.

● **Tip:** Be an active learner – join in the discussions and, as with lectures, be prepared! Know what you are supposed to be doing – and do it.

Tutorial

(Appears to be less common now – though some universities are reintroducing them to encourage a sense of 'belonging'.) Typical tutorial structure is one tutor plus two to five students. Tutorials may be based around a topic or theme or an activity. You might be asked to read an article and comment upon it. You may be expected to deliver a short presentation on a topic (see Chapter 9). As with the seminar, the tutorial is designed to get the student learning by actively engaging with the ideas and information that are considered vital to the topic.

There may be no 'right' answer to a particular issue, but you will be encouraged to think for yourself and to weigh up contradictory arguments on your way to synthesising information from various sources – and thus forming your own opinion (moving from surface to deep learning). As with the note on 'change', above, this might feel very uncomfortable. Often students want the tutor to give them the 'right' answer – but the tutor is trying to encourage the students to think for themselves.

● **Tip:** There is definitely no hiding place in the tutorial. If you do not attend you are missed – if you do attend your contributions or lack of them will be noted. Be prepared to join in.

Independent learning

No one thing is ever designed to give you 'all you need to know' on a topic. Lectures, seminars, tutorials and all the reading that you could possibly do are all designed to spur you on to further thought or activity – designing an experiment or a piece of independent research – even further reading. Thus there is much emphasis placed on independent learning. That is, you will be expected to follow up ideas in various ways, including reading around a subject, on your own **and on your own initiative**.

Some people are now using the term **inter-dependent learning** – this indicates that we cannot learn in a vacuum, but that all that we encounter comes in a human context. That is, we could not have access to useful texts (books, journals, internet material) without the librarian, we could not have meaningful discussions without other people – we are inter-dependent, social beings and we can benefit from this inter-dependency if we use it actively.

● **Tip:** Get a study partner. See the section on group work in Chapter 8.

Information everywhere

As an independent or an inter-dependent learner you will be expected to make use of the following:

■ **The library** – find your university library. Find where the books for your subject are kept. Make a habit of spending some time there every week. Notice the books that are available on your subject – notice when new books come in. Have a look at the books that are available on other subjects. Ideas can be inter-dependent as well. Thus if you are studying sociology, you might find useful material in the psychology section of your library. If studying literature, you might try some chemistry!

■ **The key text area** – many libraries acknowledge that there could never be enough books to satisfy all their students. So what they often do is have a special mini-library within the library proper. This may be called the Key Text Area (KTA) or something similar. Find this section of the library – see what books are kept there on your subject.

● **Tip:** If there are books that you need that are always out on loan, request that at least one copy be placed within the KTA.

- **Books** – become aware of the most up to date and useful texts on your subject. Get used to picking these off the shelves and having a quick look in the index – what is in the book? Anything useful? When will you read it?

- **Journals (periodicals)** – the most up-to-date books are always several months old by the time they are actually written and published – to keep really up to date with your subject you need to read the latest journals or periodicals.

● **Tip:** Find your subject librarian and ask them to recommend the best journals for you. Make a habit of reading them. When reading the journals, look at how arguments are constructed and look at how articles are written – this will be a model for your writing.

- **Quality press** – many subjects are covered in the quality papers in sections headed Education or Financial Issues or the Media and so on. Whilst such articles may not be academic enough for direct use, they do keep you abreast of current thought on your subject. There will be names dropped that you can then research in the books and journals.

● **Tip:** Start a **press cuttings file** for your subject. Get into the habit of looking in the papers every week and of putting relevant cuttings into your file.

- **Electronic information systems** – accessing information through the computer. You will be aware that search engines can get you to useful information on the web. You will also need to discover the best search engines and the best sites for your subject. Again, if in doubt, ask your subject librarian. Make a habit of checking the best sites and seeing what's new.

- **Networked information** – many university libraries have networked computers – this will be where certain key CD-ROMs can be accessed. Many of the journals and the quality press can also be found more easily on-line than in paper-based format. Again it is helpful to discover your subject librarian and ask them about these things. Once you have discovered which of your journals are on-line, make a habit of dipping into them and seeing what's new.

● **Tip:** Do a quick journal search putting in key words from your assignment question – see what happens.

▪ **Other sources** – television, radio, films, video- and audio-tapes – all have a role to play in your learning. Your university library may well offer access to a whole catalogue of useful material that comes in special forms. Don't limit yourself to paper-based approaches – explore all the sources of information that your institution offers.

Useful people and places around a university – people to see and things to do

From reading the above section you might now be aware that your subject librarian is a person to get to know! There are other useful people to discover at university: here we have listed some of them.

▪ **Personal tutor:** Many universities still appoint a personal tutor who is someone designated to give you pastoral support, someone who has your best interests at heart – as a person. Usually you find out who your tutor is by looking for a list on the department notice board. Once you have a name, make an appointment, go along and introduce yourself. Find out what being a personal tutor means at your university. This person can be your advocate if things go wrong for you. And they can write that glowing job reference if they know who you are. But if you have not approached them when things are going well for you, it will be difficult to approach them if things do go wrong.

● **Tip:** Find your personal tutor before a problem arises.

▪ **Academic tutor:** The academic tutor appears to be replacing the personal tutor in many institutions. The intention is still that this tutor will get to know you and will keep an eye on you. But now he or she may be responsible for helping you develop your academic literacy. Therefore formal meetings may be timetabled with this tutor – and you will be expected to attend. There may be specific activities set for these meetings. These activities will be designed either to develop your familiarity with academic practices, work towards specific assignments or just so that the tutor gets to know more about you. In either case, this means that this tutor will be in a position to represent you at Academic Boards, if there is ever any doubt about your grades, and they will be in a position to write good references for you either for work placement or for work proper.

● **Tip:** Again, our advice is, get to know your academic tutor: do not put it off – do it now!

■ **Subject librarian:** Universities usually appoint subject specialists as librarians and they have a much more important role than just putting the books back on the shelves. The subject librarian is a specialist in his or her own right. They have knowledge of the subject and they will be able to direct you towards useful books, journals and websites. Note: some universities offer special drop-in times with the subject librarians. Find out if your university does this and make a date to go to a session as soon as possible to see what goes on – and how to benefit from them.

● **Tip:** Go to your subject librarian and ask them about the books, journals, websites and CD-ROMs that will be most useful to you.

■ **Learning development and support:** Many universities these days realise that students benefit from specific advice on when, where and how to study. They may have a study skills collection in the library – they may actually have a learning development or support unit. Some units offer drop-in workshops where students can get one-to-one guidance with their assignments – they also offer study skills courses where students can learn and practise all the constituent skills they will need to succeed on their programmes of study. Find out if your university does this and see what they offer. Make a date to use the services and see what they can do for you. (Yes, this sounds like **even more work**! Well, what we have found is that this sort of investment on your part pays dividends in terms of time saved in other ways, improved grades and the ability to get more benefit from the time and effort that you are prepared to put in.)

■ **Student support services:** There are usually several ancillary services built around student life. These could be Welfare, Chaplaincy, Careers, Counselling, Dyslexia, Disability, and Work Placement Officer… Find out just exactly what your university offers and find out how you could benefit. Listed below is some information on the most common student support people.

■ **Careers:** The Careers people have up-to-date information on career opportunities, job requirements and how to plan and prepare *curriculum vitae* (c.v.). One of the most useful things that you could do would be to make an immediate appointment with the Careers people – we are talking in your first year, here, not three weeks before the end of your degree programme! Find out what employment opportunities are open to you, **now**. Get advice about how best to tailor your degree programme to the sort of career you are likely to take up. If you are on a modular degree programme, this will help you choose the best modules for the career that you want.

● **Tip:** Start collecting information for your final c.v. the moment you read this. Have a folder where you keep key bits of information about yourself – jobs you have done, your responsibilities and how you developed; courses that you have done and how you have utilised the information learned; modules that you cover – and how they fit you for a specific job... Go through this file every so often so that you always keep it up to date.

■ **Work placement:** The Work Placement people are the ones who find placements for students whilst they are still on their degree programmes. Once you know what career avenue seems best for you – see the Work Placement people. Find out how to get a placement in a suitable organisation. This is the best way of finding out whether or not you actually like the work. This gives you great experience to use both in your degree and in your c.v. – and if you make a good impression you may even find you have a job lined up whilst you are still taking your degree.

■ **Counselling services:** Most universities offer some form of confidential counselling service. If you find that you are having problems adjusting to being a student, if you are incredibly homesick or if you feel overwhelmed by things – go and see the counsellor.

Discussion: How much of the above was new information to you? How much were you aware of already? Has any of the information changed your mind about anything? What are you going to do now?

Remember: the point with learning is that you use information in some way. You might use that information to form an opinion. Here we are hoping that this information will form or inform your behaviour. We hope that you will do something with and about the above information.

Activity: Do something with the information

It is not enough just to notice bits and pieces of information – you must do something with it. Here are some suggestions about what to do with the information above:

1 Make a list of the key points noted above.

2 Make a list of the key people.

3 Set aside time in your schedule to go and do something – find the Key Text Area or the Learning Support Unit; make appointments with some of the key people noted above.

4 Set goals for each activity that you plan – why are you going to the Key Text Area or the Learning Support Unit? What will you ask the person that you have booked an appointment with? How will you know that you have got what you wanted?

Overall conclusion

So we have looked at learning and thought about it as an active process – gathering, recording, organising, understanding, remembering and using information. We used this to look briefly at surface and deep learning.

We moved on to examine the role of personal motivation in learning – and used the good and bad learning exercise as a spur to drawing up a personal learning contract for this book. Obviously if the contract works for you, you might try it on the course that you are doing at the moment!

After that we went on to look at learning in the context of formal study – paying particular attention to choosing your university – and understanding what happens at university. We went on to examine the types of study that occur in colleges and universities, paying attention to all the places to go and people to meet in order for you to get the most out of your time at university.

Finally we'd like you, the reader, to sit for a few moments and reflect on what you have read and done, why you did it – and what you feel that you have learned. Make a few notes so that you do not forget.

Review points

When reflecting on this chapter you might notice that:

- you are more aware of the processes of learning

- you will need to be an active learner to become successful

- studying is organised learning

- you know more about the different sorts of universities that exist – old and new

- you now better understand academic communities and the nature of studying

- you now know the sorts of activities that go on in universities and colleges

- you are now ready to make the most of your time at university

- you have engaged with various activities, which have reinforced your understanding of the different parts of the chapter.

Further reading

Tutors reading this book might like to have a look at:
Devine, T.G. (1987) *Teaching study skills*, Allyn and Bacon

2 How to organise yourself for study

Aims

To prepare you for successful academic study by examining motivation, time and organisation and time management issues.

Learning outcomes

That after reading through this chapter, and engaging with the activities, you will have:

- considered the impact of personal motivation with respect to study success

- realised the time commitment necessary for developing effective study skills

- explored organisation and time management issues

- started the process of organising yourself for effective study

- engaged with various activities that have reinforced your understanding of the different parts of the chapter.

Activity

In Chapter 1 we asked you to complete a personal study skills review. This review was to get you thinking about the sort of student that you believe you are now. It also gets you thinking about the sorts of skills that you already have – and those that you might like to develop or improve. If you have not already completed the skills review, why not do it now?

Introduction

'How to organise yourself for study' is based on the premise that studying is not about being born a good student – or even about the sort of brain capacity that you have. Being a good student is made up of all sorts of study and academic skills and practices that can be learned, rehearsed and developed.

The sorts of things that we will be looking at here are organisation and time management; targeted research and active reading will be covered in Chapter 3; memory, learning style, revision and exam techniques will be covered in Chapter 5; we will be looking at notemaking in Chapter 6 and essay writing and presentation giving in Chapter 9.

It's obvious really!

The secret with becoming a successful student, as with many of the things that we do in life, is twofold – first you must **want** to develop the relevant skills, strategies and techniques, second you must be prepared to practise, practise, practise. Nothing that we want to do just happens. It all takes time and practice.

Compare becoming a successful student with learning to drive. If this were a driving theory book, it would not mean that you would read it once and then expect to rush out and drive a car perfectly. You would expect to have many practical driving experiences as well. In these practice sessions you would be putting driving theory into practice. You would expect to make many mistakes as you practised but over time you would expect to sort them out and get better at driving.

Even when you passed your test you would still realise, hopefully, that you are always developing as a driver. There would never be a moment when you thought 'Now I am a perfect driver!' Each time you got into the car you would be practising and enhancing your driving skills. The more you made yourself aware of that (Today I learned a better way of entering and leaving a roundabout – I must remember to do that tomorrow) the better a driver you would become.

It is the same with being a student. It never stops getting better. Though there may be days when we slip back into old, less effective habits, we can always refine our techniques and get better. The writers of this book have been students and teachers for more than 25 years each. We both still expect to pick up new tips and tricks that will help us become even more effective. We still expect to refine our academic practice.

The aim of this book is to pass on successful techniques to you the reader. But remember this is not a one-stop quick fix. The study and academic skills and practices that are covered here will be part of your life for some time – and they will be things that you rehearse and develop over time. So, make your study techniques conscious – and keep practising, refining and reviewing your techniques. This way you will be able to keep improving as a student.

As before, we would like to remind you to be prepared to make mistakes and learn from them. This is the way that we learn as human beings. Maybe it feels uncomfortable to make mistakes – it makes us feel foolish. But if we can get over that, everything else gets better. There are only two big mistakes:

1 To be so frightened of making mistakes that we never do anything.

2 Not to learn from our mistakes.

So – good luck with this chapter. And remember, before you work through each of the sections, think first:

■ What do I already know about this topic?

■ What do I want from this section?

And at the end pause and reflect:

■ What have I learned?

■ How will it help me?

Organisation and time management

We are going to reflect on the personal skills review questionnaire (Chapter 1) in order to lead you into the section. We will not always do this, but it is something that you can do for yourself as you work through the book. We will move on to consider briefly the skills that you bring with you to studying. Finally we will go on to discuss when, where and how to study.

Time and commitment

In the skills review we asked you two sets of questions designed to get you thinking about some of the issues related to organisation and time management. We are going to have another look at those here.

> The first asked: 'How positive and committed are you to developing your skills? What are you prepared to do to improve? How much time and energy are you prepared to put in?'

This question is designed to get you thinking about the very real impact of **time**. It does take time to develop your skills – just as it takes time to study. One danger is thinking about all that time and saying to yourself, 'I don't have the time to learn how to study – I've got too much to do!'

Whilst this is a perfectly natural panic thought, it leads to a false economy of time. Without developing good skills, everything else takes more time, too much time. So this is a repeat encouragement – put in the time needed to start developing your skills and everything else gets easier and therefore a little quicker.

More than that – with successful strategies and practices, studying becomes more effective. This is a good thing. You have decided to be a student, which is a commitment of sorts. You are prepared to do a certain amount of work, and this is also good. This book is about getting more out of the effort that you are prepared to put in.

The second thing touched upon in this question was your motivation and commitment. You must want to develop your skills. We looked at motivation in Chapter 1 but a quick statement of the obvious here: if you do not want to develop your skills then you won't. It is as simple as that. If you do want to, then you must be prepared to invest some time in yourself (yes – time again!). And you must try to feel good about that – try to enjoy it. The less it seems like hard work and an awful chore, the better it becomes. Try to think:

- I am enjoying this.

- I can really see the point of this.

- This is working for me right now!

This might not be your normal thinking habit (maybe you are more used to thinking, what am I doing this for? This is all taking too long! This will never work for me!). But try the positive thoughts above for a change and see if it makes a difference.

The skills you bring with you

The second relevant review question asked: 'How organised are you? (If you have already brought up a family or juggled work with a hobby you are most probably already used to organising your life to make the most of your time. These are really useful transferable skills.) If you have studied before did you have set times to work? Do you have a place to study? What do you need here?'

This question was trying to do at least two things – first, to remind you that you do not come to study, to being a student and/or to this book, empty! You have already learned many things in your life. You have already developed many skills. Many of those skills will be useful to you here. It is all too easy to focus only on the things that we do not have – on our weaknesses and our failings! Not only is this not the complete picture – it can be very demoralising. Try and realise just how good you already are. This will help you become conscious of the skills that you already have – and it will give you some confidence.

Then try to think about how to adapt the skills that you already have so that they are really helpful to you in your studies. This makes you an active and proactive learner – and we have already said that the more active we are in our studies the more we learn.

So what else was that question trying to do? Well, you may have noticed that it touched upon having set times to study and having a place to study. This leads us into our section on organisation and time management proper. We have sub-headed this, when, where and how to study.

Do it! Review it!

As always, the advice given below will only work if put into practice. But much of it is there to be played with and adapted to suit you. So read through, note the useful points and try them out. After a while, review how they are working for you and adapt them so that they become more tailored to the sort of student that you are – and thus more effective.

When, where and how to study

Starting at the very beginning, a very basic good study technique is being able to organise ourselves for study – to get mentally and physically prepared for study. Organisation is widely thought to be the key to success in business, even in life itself, let alone in studying. Now this is fine if you already see yourself as an organised person – but a bit of a blow if you feel that you are chaotic and disorganised. However, there are various ways of being organised and here we are not talking about being neat and tidy – nor are we necessarily talking about making lists (though they can help!). Everybody has a slightly different learning style, so different things will work for different people. But here we are going to discuss having a time, a place and a set of techniques designed to help you study.

When

Studying is often really hard work – there is reading to do, notes to make and learn, essays and other assignments to plan, prepare and produce. Far from feeling fun and exciting, sometimes this can feel really overwhelming – sometimes it even feels quite frightening. We can work to overcome this by doing a little bit of work each day. We can read, make notes, plan an assignment, draft a sample paragraph. This can all happen over time – and having study timetables can help. However, several things can hinder working in this way.

I can only work under pressure of a deadline

There are many students who cannot start work until a deadline really frightens them. In learning development workshops at our university, students will rush up asking us to look at their essay draft quickly because it has to be handed in in half an hour!

No matter what useful comments we might make, these students have not left any time to act on that advice. Further, because they have not paced themselves properly – over a whole term, semester or year – they have not given themselves the time to understand new material, to extend their learning with additional research and to plan, prepare and refine the assignment.

These students never give themselves the time to do themselves justice. Their work never reflects what they are capable of. They never get to feel good about themselves as students.

It all seems too much, I just can't start!

Studying can feel like climbing a mountain. But there is more than one way to face a mountain! For some a mountain is so large and dangerous that they are afraid of it. For some a mountain is an exciting challenge. For some a mountain is just a thing to be tackled sensibly one step at a time. How do you view the mountain? Whatever your normal attitude, try to approach the mountain – and your assignments – one step at a time.

If you feel that it is all so overwhelming that you cannot even begin your work – try out the information on organising your time and also see the section in Chapter 6 on creativity – this will give you ideas on how to start assignments.

But I never seem to feel like working!

This statement seems to hold the essence of the old romantic notion of the artist who sits and waits for inspiration to strike. This didn't work for the artist – and it doesn't work for the student.

Nobody leaps out of bed in the morning going 'Wheee – this is the day that I tackle that huge assignment!' So do not rely on 'feeling' like studying! You have to put a study system in place.

Whilst schools do set homework and colleges and universities give reading lists and set assignment deadlines, every student has to work out for themselves just how much time they are prepared to give to their studies. They have to decide how much work they are prepared to put in, to get the results – in crude terms the grades – that they want.

So when should I study?

When studying a good rule of thumb is to build up to one-hour study periods and then to take a break. The second rule is to plan a whole host of timetables.

When planning out your timetables think about:

- Whether you are a morning, afternoon or evening person. Try to fit your study times around your maximum performance times. Work with your strengths.

- How much time you would like to give to friends and family. Your studies are important – but most of us would like to have friends and family still talking to us when our studies are over!

- How much time you have to give to work and/or chores. These days we need to earn money whilst we study. We need to keep our homes at least sanitary. Watch out though – work, housework and all chores can become excellent excuses for not working. They become displacement activities – sometimes it feels as though it is easier to completely re-build the house rather than write an essay!

- Whether you will be able to keep all your hobbies and interests going. Do you fight to keep your hobbies now – or do you plan to take them up again after your studies? Do you acknowledge time limits and decide that in the short term your studies become your hobbies? Or can you juggle time effectively and so fit more in?

- Time for rest and relaxation. As we have said studying is hard work – it can also be very stressful. It is important to get sufficient rest whilst you study and it is useful to build stress relief activities – dancing, exercise, homeopathy, massage, yoga – into your timetables right at the beginning of your studies.

■ Timetables. Timetables give you a strong guide to your work – if you keep to them. But more than that: without timetables you may feel that every time you are not working or spending quality time with friends and family you ought to be studying. You may not do that studying, but you worry – and this is exhausting in itself. Eventually it may feel that your whole life is work, work, work. Something will have to go – and it could be your studies!

Timetables to think about

■ **Study timetable:** this is a 24/7 timetable (twenty-four hours a day, seven days a week) that covers how many hours per day go to non-study – and how many go to your studies. It is where you can plan which subjects to study – and for how long. It takes some trial and error and experiment to get this right – so do give it that time.

■ **Assignment timetable:** this is a record of all the assignment deadlines that are coming up either in a term, a semester or across a whole year. Fill in deadlines and pin up on your wall – **and** place in your folder and diary. Never let a deadline take you by surprise.

■ **Exam timetable:** similar to the assignment timetable, this is a record of all the exams you will be taking. Note dates, times and locations. It is all too easy to turn up at the wrong time, on the wrong day and in the wrong place!

■ **Revision timetable:** at the appropriate time, each student should devise their own revision timetable where they work out when they are going to test their knowledge and practise for the exams that they are going to sit (more on this below).

● **Tip:** Photocopy the timetables below – play around with using them to help you focus on your work and get the most from your time.

Activity: Filling in the 24/7

Below there are two blank 24-hour timetables.

1   Fill in the first one, indicating when you expect to work, sleep, do chores and so forth. Think about the time that you have left. Put in times for study and relaxation. Think about it – are you being realistic? Make sure that you are not under- or over-working yourself. Run that programme for a few weeks.

2   After a while review your success in keeping to the study times that you set and in achieving the goals that you had in mind.

3   Change your timetable to fit in with reality! Use the second blank timetable for this.

4   Remember to do this every term, semester, year.

Keeping a timetable

Mark in the following details:

● **Tip:** Use a colour code

▨ time which must be spent in college

▨ time spent travelling

▨ personal/family commitments (children, shopping ...)

▨ any important, regular social commitments

▨ hours of sleep required.

▨ time for independent study.

Time	MONDAY	TUESDAY	WEDNESDAY	THURSDAY	FRIDAY	SATURDAY	SUNDAY
1.00							
2.00							
3.00							
4.00							
5.00							
6.00							
7.00							
8.00							
9.00							
10.00							
11.00							
2.00							
13.00							
4.00							
15.00							
6.00							
17.00							
18.00							
19.00							
0.00							
21.00							
22.00							
23.00							
4.00							

Time	MONDAY	TUESDAY	WEDNESDAY	THURSDAY	FRIDAY	SATURDAY	SUNDAY
1.00							
2.00							
3.00							
4.00							
5.00							
6.00							
7.00							
8.00							
9.00							
10.00							
11.00							
12.00							
13.00							
14.00							
15.00							
16.00							
17.00							
18.00							
19.00							
20.00							
21.00							
22.00							
23.00							
24.00							

Figure 2.1 Blank 24-hour timetables

EVENTS AND DEADLINES				
Write down the dates of the following events each term:				
	Course 1	Course 2	Course 3	Course 4
Course title:				
Exam(s)				
Essay deadline(s)				
Laboratory report deadline(s)				
Seminar presentations				
Field trips/visits				
Project report or exhibition deadlines				
Bank holidays or other 'days off'				
Other events (specify)				

Figure 2.2 Events and deadlines calendar

Term Plan – what is happening over your term/semester?							
	Mon	Tue	Wed	Thurs	Fri	Sat	Sun
Week 1							
Week 2							
Week 3							
Week 4							
Week 5							
Week 6							
Week 7							
Week 8							
Week 9							
Week 10							
Week 11							
Week 12							
Longer term deadlines:							

Figure 2.3 Term plan

Keep a WEEKLY PLAN – key events and activities each week							
Week Number:	Mon	Tue	Wed	Thurs	Fri	Sat	Sun
8am							
9am							
10am							
11am							
12noon							
1pm							
2pm							
3pm							
4pm							
5pm							
6pm							
7pm							
8pm							
9pm							
10pm							
11pm							
12midnight							
1am							

Figure 2.4 Weekly plan

Where

Everyone deserves a nice place to study, but real life is not always as convenient as that and sometimes we just have to adapt what we have and make it as near to what we need as possible. But, just as it is important that you decide when to study – and work at it until you get it right for you – it is important that you work out where you are going to study and you make that place work for you. With most of these things there is no right or wrong, there is only what works for you. So take the time to find out what **does** work for you. There are some things that you may need to think about though.

Your study space

A good place to study does not necessarily mean a completely quiet place – some people really do work best with a little bit of background noise going on – as long as it remains background.

You will need space to lay out your work, pin up your timetables, deadlines and notes. You will benefit from having your textbooks out and visible. Not only are these useful organisational things – they also help you to feel like a student.

You may need to negotiate a space with family or flatmates: your studies are part of your life now – and they must fit in. Sorting out a study space may help everyone in your life – including **you** – realise just how important your studies are.

You may need to experiment with working at home or in the library. You may find that you do your best studying as you travel – and suddenly being a commuter adds ten hours of study time to your week, if you take your books with you.

Whether you want to work in a library or on a bus, you will also need a study space at home. A place where you really do stick up those timetables and those notes. Where you pin up deadlines and write up all the new words that you are learning, so that you revise them every time you walk past.

Ideally it would be a place that is permanently your study space so that you can leave your work out rather than having to tidy it away at the end of each study session. However, if this is not possible, maybe have a large plastic box – put all your work into this at the end of a study session and slip it under your bed till the next time. At least this way you will not keep losing things.

When studying you do need light and air – you need to see and breathe! You benefit from having subject files neatly labelled and ready to hand, this helps you to feel and become more organised. Your subject books should be visible so that you can see them – and, again, feel like a student.

You need pens and pencils to hand, also highlighters, a stapler and staples, paper clips, correction fluid, Post-its, coloured pens – and all sorts of different sizes of paper. All these resources make it easier to write notes, annotate source material, mark important pages in books and so forth. The different sized paper gives you paper to make notes on, paper to make plans on, paper to print work on. Further, if you play around with materials and colour, you feel an injection of energy and enthusiasm – and this just makes the job easier.

You would also benefit from having a computer! A computer makes it easier to word process work so that it looks nice – and makes it easier for the tutor to read and mark. More than that, it makes it possible to draft and redraft work till you get it right.

These days the computer also allows you access to research materials on the Internet: you must have at least seen the BBC adverts for all its teaching support sites – well, there are loads of them out there. Further there are many CD-ROMs designed to help your studies – there is much more to the CD-ROM than a computer game. Also, most schools, colleges and universities have websites that contain useful information. Not only that, many courses these days are supported by on-line materials – even interactive sites for testing information. Make use of these.

● **Tip:** Having your own computer is even more important than having a pen!

Remember to make that study space work for you. Get into the habit of giving 100% whenever you sit down to study. Act as if you and your studies are important – they are, and so are you. So, once you have a study space sorted out you should practise using it positively. Say to yourself as you sit down: 'Now I am working', 'I enjoy being a student.' Try to avoid those old negative thoughts: I don't want to be here. This is too hard. I'd rather be… Negative thoughts have a negative effect – positive thoughts have a positive effect.

Having that study space

Here are some comments from other students:

- It felt really good having my own study space. It made me feel like a real student.

- I felt that at last I could settle down to some real work.

- I felt a bit frightened at first – you know? Like now I couldn't put it off any longer! I'd have to take it seriously.

- Sometimes I use my space to sort of trick myself into working. I think, I'll just sit there for a minute… Next thing I know I've been working away for an hour and I feel really good.

■ I felt guilty at having to cut myself off from the kids. It just felt so selfish. I have to work really hard at still giving them some time.

■ I used to get so frustrated; it was like every time I sat down to work they would start demanding things from me. Now we all sit down to work at the same time – even if they are just crayoning or reading a storybook. This has helped us all feel better.

■ I still like going to the library to work – but it's great having a proper place for my stuff at home. It really does help.

Activity: Sorting out a study space

1   If you have not already done so, sort out a place to study. Make sure that you can use this space at the times that you have planned to study in your timetable.

2   Over time, collect the resources that we have mentioned above.

3   In the meantime, make a list of all the resources that you need. What materials do you have already? Which ones are you going to buy? Which books can you get easily from the library? Which ones are so important that you ought to buy them? How many can you afford? Etc.

Give me some space

As you can see, there is no right or wrong response to having your own study space. For each of us there is only our reaction – and what we choose to do about it!

If having your own space makes you feel like a 'proper' student (and there is no one model of what a 'proper' student is!) then you will only have to sit at your table or desk to put yourself in the right mood to study. You can always do what one of the other students (above) does and sometimes 'trick' yourself into getting some work done.

If it makes you feel a bit frightened, console yourself. New experiences are often frightening, at first! It might help to say to yourself several times, I am a proper student, each time that you sit down to study.

If your family always chooses that moment to want you – again, do what the other student did, and try to get them to 'study' at the same time as you. Depending on their age, this might mean real study – in which case the tips in the book will also help them! Or it could be 'nearly study' if they are very young. If that will not work with your lot, you may have to wait until they are in bed to study. Whatever works for you.

How to study

This is the longest section and it will cross-reference with information that you will be getting in other parts of this book. The whole book is also designed to get you studying in more successful ways. However, here are some practical tips on how to study.

Want it: Everyone should know what he or she is studying and why. Make sure that you do know what you want from each course that you are studying – and how your life will be changed when you reach your goals.

● **Tip:** Remember to write your goals on those Post-its and stick them up in your study space. Fill in your learning contract for each course, module or unit that you do.

Get the overview: (also in Chapter 4) when on a course do not drift from week to week wondering what's going on. Work out how the course has been put together. Know how the course is being assessed. Read the assignment question at the beginning of the course, not the end. If there are to be exams – check out past papers at the beginning of your studies, not the end. All this gives you a sense of how the course has been put together and where you are going each week.

Epistemology: We mentioned this in the first chapter. Remember every course has its own theory of knowledge – what counts as argument and evidence for your subject. Make sure you know the what, why and how of all your subjects. If in doubt, ask!

● **Tip:** Read the journals to get a model of how to argue and write in your subject. Use a dictionary and a subject dictionary.

Be positive: Just as an athlete will perform better if they feel like a success and think positive thoughts, so a student will learn more if they can adopt positive attitudes and develop self confidence.

● **Tip:** When your motivation runs low, role-play, or act like, a successful student.

Timing: Set those study timetables in motion. Remember, work for an hour then take a break. A short break will recharge your batteries and make your work profitable. Sometimes people feel that a student is someone who sits in the same place for hours struggling with hard work. This belief can make you very frustrated, angry and tired – but it rarely produces good work.

■ **Time tips:** Research indicates that we concentrate best in **15-minute bursts**. This means that sitting down to a seven hour study period might not be the most effective way to work. We might sit there for hours – but not much work is getting done! When we study we have to get into the habit of regularly recharging our mental batteries to restore our interest in what we are doing and thus to benefit from the activity. We can do this by:

■ taking a short rest

■ changing what we do

■ making the task very important

■ making the task interesting, stimulating or more difficult.

Use the time: We both know students who sit down to study – out come the pens and paper – they get rearranged. Out come the books and the highlighters – they get rearranged. They go for a coffee. They go for a glass of water. They put one lot of books away and get out another set. They look at the clock – oh good! An hour has passed – they put their materials away. But they have done no work! Watch out for this.

● **Tip:** Goal setting will help you benefit from independent study time.

Goal set: Before you sit down to study, set yourself some goals. Know what you are doing and why. So do not just start reading a book because it is on the reading list. Know why you are reading a section of that book. If you are not sure – have a look at the assignment question and find a bit of the book that will help you with a bit of the assignment. Then you will know what you are doing and why. This makes all the difference.

One worry at a time

One thing that can stop people achieving enough when they sit down to work is too much worry. They sit down to write an essay – and worry about the two other essays that they also have to write. They worry about the weather or the bills. They worry about anything and everything. If we worry about everything – we do nothing. One of the hardest tricks to being a successful student is to learn how to worry about one thing at a time.

It is as if we need to set up a set of shelves in our brain. Put all our different worries on the shelves. Learn to take down one thing at a time and give it our total concentration. When we have finished with that, put it back on the shelf and take down something else.

Like everything else recommended in this book, this is a skill that has to be learned and developed through practice.

Be active: when studying independently be just as active as when you are in a lecture or joining in a class discussion. Read actively, asking questions as you go (more on this below). Think about the information that you are receiving – what does it mean? Do you understand it? If not, what are you going to do about that? How does it connect with what you already know (things that you have heard in class or read in other places)? Connecting up information in this way is a really important part of active learning. Make active notes – typically, **key word** notes – in patterns (more on this in Chapter 6). Revise those notes actively.

Review actively: At the end of each study session – independent study or a lecture or class – take some time to reflect on what you have read or heard. Check what you have done. Recall what you have learned. Make brief notes to make the learning conscious (see Chapter 10).

Study partners and groups: Study is best when undertaken actively – this is where a study partner or a study group can be invaluable. Talking over new information with other people is the easiest way to understand and learn it – to make it your own. Further, if you encounter a problem you can talk to (or phone) your partner. Probably they will not know the solution either. Oh the relief! You are not alone and you are not stupid! Then the situation changes as you work on the problem and sort it out together.

Don't end on a sour note: Try not to end a study session on a problem – it is de-motivating and it can make it that little bit harder to start studying again. Make use of your study partner. Speak to them – talk it over. If that is not possible, you can always make a note of the problem and sleep on it – sometimes this does work and you find the solution comes to you when you wake up. What you do not want to do though is go to bed so worried about the problem that you lie there fretting about it all night – you still do not solve the problem and you have made everything worse by losing sleep and gaining stress.

Relaxation and stress relief: Remember to make time to rest, relax and let go of stress. This is important. You need rest to carry on. Stress relief allows you to let go of tension – and this helps you to perform better. When we are stressed our body releases cortisol – a hormone that has a direct impact on the brain causing the cortex to shrink. Further stress releases adrenalin, the flight or fight hormone. The combination of these hormones produces the narrow, tunnel vision necessary for fight or flight – and our brains lose their short-term memory capacity. These conditions might save our lives when escaping from a burning building, but they work against us being able to study successfully. When studying we need to be relaxed to utilise our short-term memory and to develop a breadth and depth of vision.

Conclusion

In this section we have considered some basic organisation and time management techniques via a discussion of when, where and how to study. Remember, though, that none of this will mean anything unless and until you put the ideas into practice. If it seems too difficult to put them all into practice at once sort out one thing at a time. As you do this, take the time to reflect on how the things that you are doing are working for you. If something is not working – or stops working – change it. These tips work best once you adapt them to suit yourself.

Review points

When you reflect on this chapter you might notice that you have:

- considered the impact of personal motivation on study success

- realised the time commitment necessary for developing effective study skills and academic practices

- explored organisation and time management issues

- started the process of organising yourself for effective study

- engaged with various activities that have reinforced your understanding of the different parts of the chapter.

3 How to research and read academically

Aims

To prepare you for successful academic study by examining targeted research and active reading skills.

Learning outcomes

That after reading through this chapter, and engaging with the activities set, you will have:

- gained an understanding of the nature of research
- gained an understanding of the purpose of reading
- gained an understanding of targeted research and active reading strategies
- engaged with various activities that have reinforced your understanding of the different parts of the chapter.

Introduction

As a student, people will always be telling you to read; more than that, people will be expecting you to 'read around a subject' without being told. But this is another one of those skills or practices that we are not just born with – so this chapter is designed to help you to organise your research and to benefit from your reading. We will get you thinking about issues like – what is research? Why do we read? How can I read effectively? It is an important section and we hope that you find it useful. As always, before you start think quickly:

■ What do I already know on this topic?

■ What do I need to find out?

■ How will knowing this make me a more successful student?

Research and reading skills

Research

Many people think of research as something special and different – something 'other', something extra that they will do on top of their class work. But research is about investigating or searching for ideas to increase your knowledge.

In this context, all of your studies constitute research for you. Listening in class and/or lectures, reading textbooks and journals – all involve research for they are all opportunities for you to engage with the theories and knowledge claims that already exist in your subject area. And you engage with these existing ideas so that you can gather ideas and information to deepen your own understanding. Eventually you will use what you have gathered to construct your own arguments – often in class discussion, seminars and tutorials – and also in your assignments.

Primary and secondary sources

When asking people for research data (information) we often talk about using primary and secondary sources. As the names imply **primary** means first hand and **secondary** means 'second hand' – that is, moving away from primary data to the arguments and opinions that people have drawn by using primary evidence. Things to think about:

Primary sources

■ Original documents – e.g. birth certificates, treaties, and testimonies – might be used in History.

■ One's own observations – for example, if training to be a teacher, you would note what students actually **do** in the classroom, and attempt to analyse it.

■ One's own investigations – for example, Science practicals or using questionnaires or interview techniques to gather data for almost any subject.

- Case studies – for example, in Business Studies, students will often be given an account of a real life business venture or in Social Sciences an account of a real life scenario. The student is supposed to analyse the case study using theories covered on the course.

- Poetry and novels – for example, in Literature Studies, the poetry and prose that is actually studied constitutes primary material. (Critics produce secondary source material.)

- Films and television programmes can be primary sources in Media or Film Studies – but might constitute secondary sources if used for evidence as part of other subjects, Sociology for example.

Secondary sources

- Write ups of other people's observations, experiments, interviews and questionnaires become secondary sources for you.

- The subject literature – articles, chapters, textbooks where people write up their arguments – are all secondary sources.

Targeted research and active reading

When we talk about targeted research and active reading we are focusing on the notion of the active learner in control of their own learning. In particular we are focusing here on a systematic research and read strategy. But first, let us look at reading in some detail.

Looking at reading

We are a literate society and we engage in lots of reading. Even people who would not consider themselves to be readers will read newspapers, magazines, recipes, knitting patterns, the television pages, light fiction like Mills and Boon romances or detective stories. Obviously, once we talk about reading in the context of being a student we are normally talking about another sort of reading material and another sort of reading strategy, and that is what we shall cover here in depth. But this does not mean that all your current reading strategies are irrelevant – it might mean simply that they need adapting to become more effective to your needs as a student.

Activity: Using your college library

Introduction to the library

Find your college library. If you find it an intimidating place hopefully this worksheet will take you through the library in a useful way so that you start using as much of the library as possible, as soon as possible – and it will not be intimidating any more.

For each activity, tick the box when you have completed it, and write in details where indicated.

Books Find the part of the library that houses the books for your subject.
▨ My books are ....
▨ Write in the Dewey decimal number (the numbers on the spine of the book) for your subject..

Journals
▨ When studying it is important to read the relevant journals for your subject. Where are your journals kept? ....
▨ Write in the title of two journals that you could be reading:
　Journal one..
　Journal two..

Newspapers
▨ With most subjects it is also important to read the 'quality' press. Where are the newspapers kept?...

Key text area (counter loans)
▨ The key text area holds the most important texts for each subject – find it. My key text area is ....

Study areas What facilities are there for independent study in your library?
▨ My library offers quiet study areas?...
▨ My library offers group study areas?.......................................

Workshops Some libraries contain student help workshops – does yours?
▨ My library does/does not have workshops.
▨ They are located ....
▨ Opening times are ....

Now that you have had a quick introduction to the library, list three things that you like about it:
1 ....
2 ....
3 ....

What would you tell someone else about the library?
1 ....
2 ....

Activity: Thinking about reading

Before we go into our research and reading technique in detail, reflect on the skills review question that asked you to reflect on your reading:

> What sorts of reading do you do at the moment (e.g. newspapers, light fiction, knitting patterns, etc.)? Are you happy with your reading skills? What do you need here?

Did you make notes on this? It is a good idea to make these sorts of 'brainstorming' notes very short – go for one or two word memory joggers that you can refer back to later to see if your goals have been met.

Why don't you compare your responses with those of another student given below?

Responses from another student:

- Read newspapers and magazines.

- I am critical.

- I worry whether or not I will understand my academic reading – it's not a comic, is it?

- I want to know how to develop my understanding – and how to get information from difficult books.

Query: Were these responses anything like yours? Do you notice anything about them?

Discussion: If the responses above were like your own, they appear to have highlighted quite a common student fear – that as students you will find the reading difficult and that you feel that you are not yet qualified to select relevant information when reading. At the very least, this should reassure you that you are not alone in your fears and concerns.

Another thing that we noticed was that where the student was confident about what he was saying, his notes were short – but where he started to move onto unfamiliar territory (his fears and concerns) his notes become longer and longer. It is as if here he does not quite trust himself to remember his points.

This is an important thing to notice with respect to notemaking. We will repeatedly be asking you to make short, key word notes. Yet, typically, when you feel uncertain of the information you will be reluctant to trust short notes.

● **Tip:** Write your notes in stages – write sentences first and reduce to keywords as your confidence in a topic increases. We will refer to this again in Chapter 6.

It's all too much

One thing that does seem to put students off academic reading is the sheer amount of reading that they feel they will have to do. A quick visit to the library reveals thousands of books – and then there are journals and newspapers and the Internet! It is not surprising that this intimidates many people. Then they start to read an academic text, perhaps for the first time – and it all takes so long! There will never be enough time to do all that reading – and this can really put people off even starting to read. Another problem is that people really do not understand why they have been asked to read – what is the point of it anyway?

Why read?

So why does a student read? One answer to this might be – because they are told to! And this might be true, but there is a purpose to academic reading. Remember the points made in Chapter 1, above, about the first stage of learning, which is gathering new ideas and information (performing our research). When we study we are adding to the sum of our own knowledge on a topic – and this is the point of academic reading.

Reading around the subject

Whilst you are given information in lectures, classes, seminars and tutorials, this will never be 'all you need to know' on a subject. You are also supposed to develop your knowledge of the subject beyond what the tutor has told you – thus you have to read about the subject. This means that you will have to read what other thinkers and experts have to say – to read the latest journal articles – and to see how the subject is covered in the serious newspapers.

From novice to initiate

Thus reading is about gathering information to build on and extend your subject knowledge. You will typically be making notes of that information in the expectation of using it in your thinking, in your essays, presentations and exams – at all stages of your student life. And, if it is true that we start student life as a novice but expect to leave the subject as an initiate (one who now does know the subject), then we might need to do very different sorts of reading as we pass through the different stages of our student life.

The novice – starting to read on a subject

For example, if you are just beginning to study a topic, you may know very little about it at all. Thus the first sort of reading that you do might be general reading on the topic. With this reading you are trying to understand the topic and may have many doubts, fears and questions:

■ What is this subject about?

■ What are the basic things that I ought to know and understand about the topic?

■ Who are the people that I ought to read?

This is why tutors put **reading lists** together for students. This gives a clue as to 'who' you should be reading – and what.

Activity: Thinking about your subject

Answer the following questions about yourself and your studies:

1 Why are **you** studying your subject?

2 What do you know about the subject already?

3 What do you need to know? (What will you be tested on in your assignments and final exams?)

4 What counts as argument and evidence in your subject?

5 What reading have you done before on the topic?

6 Who should you be reading now on the topic? (Check out your Reading List.)

Comment: Without knowing the answers to most of these questions, we can wander around our reading slightly lost, never quite understanding the point of it.

However, when we first start studying a subject, we may not even know that we should be asking these questions – let alone trying to answer them!

It seems so hard

Being a novice in a subject means that the first reading that you do on your topic can be the most difficult. It is not necessarily that it really is difficult – it is just that because you are new to the subject it all feels new and uncertain to you. Fortunately it does get much easier after this!

Extending your knowledge

So, if the first stage of reading that you do is to gain a general understanding of your subject – that is, an awareness of its knowledge base, key people and academic practice – the next stage is to extend your understanding. This is where you really get to grips with your 'reading around the topic'. That is, if your lecturer covers something in class, you might go to a textbook or journal to see what other people have said on that subject. Here you might move from the generally accepted wisdom in the area to the more radical ideas or the more contested claims.

Becoming an initiate

However, whilst the ideas that you encounter might be increasing in complexity, the task is getting easier for you, because you are adding to or challenging what you already know. You are not starting from scratch but you are building on what you know about the subject. Further, as well as encountering new people and new ideas, you are also encountering ideas that you have met before and you are reading people – or about people – that you have encountered before so a sense of familiarity is building up.

For example, if this is the first Study Skills book that you have ever read – all this might be new to you. But if you now pick up another Study Skills book and go to their section on reading, you will be able to see if what they say agrees with what is written here. If it is different, you might ask yourself why. This might even prompt you to look at yet another Study Skills book to see what they say – and so on.

This is the basic principle of academic reading. You start reading to gain an understanding – you then build and build and build. You look for arguments that say one thing, and arguments that say something different. Your goal is to develop your knowledge and understanding as you bring the differing arguments together in your own mind (and this is where your writing comes in).

I hope that we have now made a good case for why you have to read when you study a subject. Let us now move on to our reading system which is an active reading system that gives advice on targeting your reading, setting goals for that reading and also on how to read as effectively and successfully as possible.

Make a meal of it – use the QOOQRRR

Active reading is more than passing your eyes over the page, it is even more than writing down everything that you read – it is about interacting with a text as you read it, and it may be a new technique for you as a student. The QOOQRRR (pronounced *cooker*) technique is a system that promotes active reading – from the very selection of what to read, through the goal setting that you do before you start reading it, to the questions that you ask as you read. QOOQRRR stands for Question, Overview, Overview, Question, Read, Re-read and Review. We will look at each of these in turn.

Question – reading with a purpose

Let us start with the first Question – this is about targeting your reading: it is about reading with a purpose – having specific goals – and using these to help you to choose what to read very carefully.

So, before you start to read something you should know exactly why you are reading it. It is not about choosing the first book on the reading list and ploughing through it from beginning to end without any clear goals in mind. If you have already tried to do that you will know that it is neither a happy nor a productive exercise!

But why am I reading NOW?

So, what should you do? The first thing to do is to know why you are reading the text in the first place. You need to know where your reading is going; you have to know what you are looking for. You need specific goals each time you read – see box.

Why do we read?

There are many possible goals for your reading: here are a few:

- You may read something to gain an overview of a topic that is new for you.

- You may read to discover the point of view of that person your lecturer keeps talking about.

- You may be reading to find someone or something that disagrees with that person the lecturer keeps talking about.

- You may be reading to find one quote that will finish off a paragraph that you have already written.

- You may be reading to find 'evidence' for every single part of your assignment.

There is no single reason to read, as we keep reminding you, there is only *your* reason to read – and making sure that you do know what that is. Knowing why you are reading can lead to successful reading – and it can help shape your notes. After all, there is no need for you to make key word notes of a whole chapter – if you are only looking for one quote. On the other hand just noting down a few quotes may not be helpful if this is the first time you have studied something and you are really looking to gain an overview of a new topic.

● **Tip:** You will be expected to do and learn many things on each course that you take: don't try to read about them all at once – look for one thing at a time.

O is for Overview

Typically this questioning goal setting habit requires learning a new reading habit first – one of skimming and scanning course information before you start to read anything at all. So instead of just picking up a book and reading it – check the course requirements first.

Gain and use an overview of each course that you are taking before you start to read. Things like course aims and learning outcomes (see also Chapter 4), the assignment question, the reading list, past exam papers – all tell you what you are supposed to do and learn to pass the course. You have to use that information to help you decide what you are looking for when you read.

The question is the key

A quick tip with reading is to approach the assignment question first. Break the question down into key words: choose one word – and plan to read around that. Then move on to another word and read around that – and so on till you have read around all the words in the question, separately.

Some people might worry that that is a very slow and cumbersome way of reading. Surely it would be better to look for the whole answer to the whole question all at once?

But they didn't write about my question!

Well, the people you are reading did not perform their research to answer your assignment questions. They may have covered something similar to what you are doing – or they might have explored something that corresponds to one part of your question – and in each case you will be able to use their work as evidence for one part of your assignment. But to find the whole answer to all of your question you will have to look for one thing at a time.

Query: Does this sound strange to you? Or does it sound like common sense?

If this does sound like a very strange way of reading to you, that indicates that you might need considerable practice before you feel comfortable with it as a system.

If it sounds like common sense to you, it may mean that you have a natural predisposition to study in this way – and the overall process may come to you more easily.

As always, there is no right or wrong type of person – there is who you are and what you choose to do to improve your own skills.

Discussion:
Now this may seem a very reductionist view of reading – maybe you have a deep and abiding passion for learning for its own sake. Maybe you love your subject so much that you are prepared to read anything and everything that you can on the topic. Well, this reading strategy does not hurt that. Evidence shows that when we read with specific goals in mind, we actually get more overall from that reading – not less!

Overview – sources of information

Before you read you need to choose what to read very carefully. Overviewing the following sources of information will help you get to the information that you want – quickly.

■ **Books:** Find some of the books on the reading list and have a look at them – do they seem easy or difficult to read? How do you know? Will you read on your own or with a study partner? When will you do this reading?

■ **Contents pages:** Look for a word from the assignment question in the Contents pages – have a look at those bits of the book. Choose small sections of the book to read. Decide when you will do the reading.

■ **Indexes:** Look for the word in the index at the back of the book. If it is mentioned, note the page numbers that are given. Go to these pages first. Once you have read these pages, decide whether or not you will read any more of that book.

■ **Wider searches:** Go to the electronic catalogue in your library – use the key word, author or subject search facilities and see what books come up – find some of them and then repeat the Contents/Index strategy with them.

■ **Using people:** Ask your tutor, other students or the subject librarian for assistance. Any of these might be able to narrow your search for you.

■ **The Internet:** As well as helping with the key word searches, your subject librarian can help you find the most useful Internet sites for your subject. The Internet is vast – and not all of the search engines are useful to you. The trick is to find the search engines that take you to useful sites. Your librarian will know this.

■ **Use the journals:** Ask your subject librarian to point you towards the most useful journals on your subject. Books are good, but, typically, once you progress from gaining a basic understanding of a subject to extending your knowledge of that subject, journals come into their own. Journals publish the most recent research; thus they will keep your research fresh and interesting. Typically universities will have actual journals and access to journals on-line. Find out – have a look – always use journals as a starting point for research.

**Activity: Get the overview of a book
(an activity that works best with a study partner)**

I   Take a book, preferably a textbook or reader, but nearly any book will do for now. Give yourself two minutes to find out what the book is about. After two minutes you are going to describe the book to someone else.

2   Give your partner two minutes with a book – and repeat the process.

Query: How did it go?

Points:

▨ Typically we use overview techniques to gather information about books.

▨ We will look at the author and see whether or not it is someone we know.

▨ If it is a textbook we might see if it is on the reading list – or written by our tutor! It is always politic to read any books that our tutors have written!

▨ If we have been studying for some time, we will recognise writers that we have read before. We can say whether or not we like his or her writing style. We can predict whether or not they will have something to say on our new assignment topic.

▨ We will look at the blurb on the back of the book and see what it tells us.

▨ We look at the contents page and decide what, if anything, looks interesting.

▨ If there is an index we scan that.

These are really useful scanning techniques to bring to your active, academic reading.

O is for Overview – choosing what to read

Once you know why you are reading – that is, you have gained an overview of your course and selected something to research, a key word from your assignment question perhaps – then you start the process of deciding what to read. There are some helpful hints in the boxes below.

**Overview: knowing what you are reading – chapters
and paragraphs**

All the above overview activities lead you **to** information. Once you have chosen something that you are going to read, you must know what it is about before you start to read it – and you must decide how much of it you are actually going to read.

▶

So, once you have a chapter of a book or a journal article in your hand, get the overview of that as well:

- Read the **introduction** (first paragraph) and **conclusion** (last paragraph): these tell you what the thing is about.

- Once you know that, you can decide whether or not you really do want to read it – and you can more clearly define why you are reading the bits that you will read.

- Read the first sentence of every **paragraph**. First sentences tell you what the paragraph is about.

- See which paragraphs are on your topic. Decide which ones you will read in depth.

- **Now** you should have a skeleton understanding of the whole chapter/article – and you have started to plot your course through the article/chapter. You are being an active learner.

Nearly there

Have you noticed all the work that we have done so far? And we haven't actually started to read yet! Well, we are still not quite ready. You may now generally know why you are reading – and you may know what you are reading – but have you set specific goals yet? This leads us on to our second Q for question.

Question

Once you have gained the overview of a specific text you may decide that you do not need to read it at all – or maybe you only need to read a chapter or a couple of pages. The key is to make decisions about which bits to read and why you are reading them.

We have already suggested that one way of setting goals for your reading is to focus on individual parts of your assignment question (the key words) and to read around one of those at a time. But once you have chosen something to read make sure you clarify your own goals – you must ask yourself **questions**:

- Why am I reading this?

- What am I looking for?

- What do I need?

- Where will I use the information?

- How will I use the information?

- Which bit of my assignment will it help me with?

- Which of the learning outcomes will it help me with?

- How will I know when I have what I need?

Once you have your questions you are ready to read.

● **Tips:**
● Write your questions down so that you can keep referring to them: this will keep you on track and active as you read.
● Choose a notemaking strategy that suits your reading purpose.

R for Read

Once you know what and why you are reading, you are ready to read. This reading is the academic reading that does seem to frighten a lot of people. No matter what your feelings are about it at the moment, we can assure you it does get better with practice. Have a look at some thoughts on reading from another student before we move on.

Thoughts on reading from another student

'That week when you did that reading session I hated that and I was really uncomfortable the whole lesson... because I was so unsure and not confident and, as I looked round, everyone seemed to be getting on with it and I thought I don't know what the hell she wants me to do.

And you know as soon as you're in that position, you can't learn anything, you can't take anything in. Things were being said, and I couldn't understand. And I was sitting with a couple of people who seemed to know what it was all about and I thought Oh crikey. You know? And it was awful. It was horrible. I didn't like that at all.'

Yet when the same student was asked later about a positive learning experience she said:

'But I was thinking about all those books on that booklist. I was thinking I had to read every single one of those books and I didn't know how I was going to manage that so I thought I'd just bluff it a bit you know.

But later on I found from you that I didn't need to do that. When you did that bit about reading – about books, I mean I wasn't aware that I didn't know anything about

▶

that first page bit, about this is the author and this is when it was published and this is where it was published. I didn't know any of that. I didn't have a clue because books have always been really alien to me you know?

And when you showed us about looking in the index and looking in the contents and then finding the bit that interests you and then going to your first paragraph and reading the first few lines and seeing if it's what you want. I found that really valuable.'

Query: What are your reactions to this student's feelings about learning how to approach an academic text? Are her reactions similar to or different from your own? Did reading this help in any way?

Comment: As tutors, we learned a lot from this student's reactions to learning how to read an academic text:

1   It was difficult.

2   The difficulty brought with it many negative feelings.

3   The negative feelings swamped everything else so that nothing could happen at that time.

4   Later the student did start to try the technique out.

5   Eventually it became one of the most useful techniques that she felt she got from the study skills programme.

Query: What does that tell you?

Discussion: So, reading can be difficult – it can even be quite frightening. Worse, **at first even learning how to read academically can be frightening!** As always, we offer the reassurance that these things do get easier with practice. Try to take comfort from the student's experiences above. She managed to move from real fear and loathing to confidence and assurance comparatively quickly. You can, too.

Reading – actively

Let us move on to consider academic reading in more depth. Once we have accepted that it is good to read, and once we have something selected to read, how can we read it effectively?

As with all active learning, academic reading requires the use of an active questioning approach. Therefore, the Q for questioning does not stop once you know why and what you are reading. When reading you need to keep asking things like – what does this mean? Who else has said that? But didn't someone else say...? And so forth. And each time you ask these questions, you should 'mark up' your text. That is, you should make some sort of note or mark on the thing that you are reading.

This is very much about being interactive with a text both mentally and physically. Thus ideally you want to be reading and making notes on your own book or a section of a library book. **Note:** you really should not get physical with other people's books – and you do have to get physical with a book to get the most from it – so photocopy the relevant pages of library books – and mark up your photocopies.

Reading resources and tips

As reading requires physical as well as mental activity from you, we recommend that you gather all your resources around you when you start to read. Things that will help:

- Have paper, pencils, pens, highlighters, paper clips, etc. to hand.

- Write your questions down. (The what I want and need questions.)

- Mark off the passage that you are actually reading. The easiest way to do this is to simply slip a piece of paper or a paper clip at the end of the section that you want to read. This gives you a physical goal – it also helps the brain to relax a little bit (phew – I can manage that much!). Without the barrier or marker it can feel like there is too much to read and this can swamp us.

- Use another piece of paper to guide your eye down the page. One of the problems with academic reading is not working with the physiology of the eye. Typically our eyes move around – as we read they dart about over the page. Often you find yourself reading the same sentence over and over again. By the time you have read it 50 times, an already difficult task has become that much harder. A piece of paper placed on the line that you are actually reading helps to bring your eye back to the correct place in the book. This alone can save you much time.

- Now read one paragraph at a time in an active, interactive way. Typically this will mean asking a series of questions of the text as we read – and making notes **on** the chapter as we go.

Interactive reading questions

Here are questions to ask as you read. Remember to be active and interactive as you read.

● **Tip:** Read one paragraph at a time, asking the questions as you go.

1 **What is the main idea here?** The main topic of a paragraph is usually revealed in the first sentence. Highlight the word or write your own word in the margin.

● **Tip:** Reading the first sentences of all the paragraphs will give you a skeleton framework of the whole piece. This is very useful for getting the overview – and extremely useful for **summary writing**.

2 **What is the author's argument?** That is what is the author saying about the topic – are they for it or against it? Again highlight the text and/or write in the margin.

● **Tip:** Think! Analyse the argument.

3 **Where is the author coming from?** Notice where the author is 'coming from' – are they on the left or the right? Are they Marxist or ecologist? Are they class-based or do they have a feminist perspective?

● **Tip:** Find out whether or not these differences are important to your academic practice. For example, this might be extremely important information on a Sociology or Literature programme, but maybe not so important on a Maths programme.

4 **Have I encountered this argument before? Where?** This gets you thinking about what you are reading – it is getting you to make connections and to make them conscious. Record your thoughts by underlining, highlighting or making key word notes in the margin.

● **Tip:** Make a note of the name of the other person or of how your tutor would respond to what you are reading.

5 **Have I encountered a different argument somewhere? Where?** Again, this is getting you to make connections – and to notice consciously the arguments that contradict or go against each other.

● **Tip:** Make a note of the person or people who say something different to what you have just read.

6 **What evidence is being offered?** Highlight, make a note. Remember that evidence is different for each subject. Make sure you know what counts as valid argument and evidence in your subject.

7 **Is the evidence valid? Why do I think it is or is not valid?** Make notes. Sometimes all you need to do is put a question mark or an

exclamation mark to show that you disagree with something – or jot down the name of the person who says something different.

● **Tip:** This does get easier with practice.

8 **How does this connect with what I have already read/heard?** Sometimes what you read will reinforce what you know or believe already; sometimes it might make you question that. Notice! Make a note.

● **Tip:** Think – now what do I think?

9 **What is the author's final point?** Usually the 'point' is in the final sentence of a paragraph. Notice what the author intended the paragraph to do.

It's a bit slow, isn't it?

As said, you should ask all those questions of one paragraph – and then move on to the next. I think you can see why it can be a slow business. Remember, though, you will not necessarily read everything in this depth, the trick is to use your overview and questioning techniques to tell you which bits you should read in-depth, and which bits you only need to skim.

Further, because you are being analytical and critical as you read, you will get more benefit from this reading – it is productive reading. So whilst you may use these techniques to read less in terms of quantity, you will get more in terms of quality from that reading.

● **Tips:**
● See this reading as an investment of time – not a problem of time.
● The only notes you should make at this stage of your reading are the notes that you scribble on the text itself – your annotations and marginalia. Anything else would be a waste of time for notes that you make too soon will be too long and passive.

R for Re-read

Once you have read your whole chosen section in this way you are ready to make your own 'to keep' notes. If we make our 'take-away' notes too soon, they may be too long; if we make them when we have really thought about the text, they can be brief and active. The trick is to construct your own key word, pattern notes of the text – using your own interactions with the text (your marginalia, highlighting and underlining) to help you.

On this re-read you are quickly glancing at the text and looking again at your own commentary. You want to use this to construct your own pattern on the text. (For detailed information on notemaking, please go to Chapter 6.)

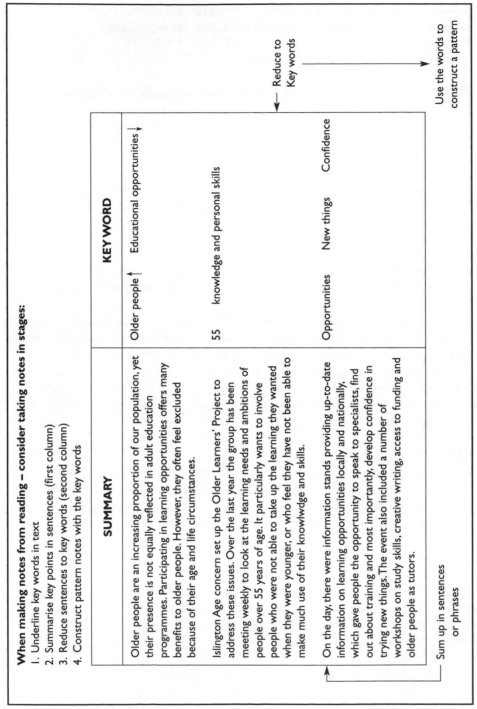

When making notes from reading – consider taking notes in stages:

1. Underline key words in text
2. Summarise key points in sentences (first column)
3. Reduce sentences to key words (second column)
4. Construct pattern notes with the key words

SUMMARY	KEY WORD
Older people are an increasing proportion of our population, yet their presence is not equally reflected in adult education programmes. Participating in learning opportunities offers many benefits to older people. However, they often feel excluded because of their age and life circumstances.	Older people ↑ Educational opportunities ↓
Islington Age concern set up the Older Learners' Project to address these issues. Over the last year the group has been meeting weekly to look at the learning needs and ambitions of people over 55 years of age. It particularly wants to involve people who were not able to take up the learning they wanted when they were younger, or who feel they have not been able to make much use of their knowlwdge and skills.	55 knowledge and personal skills
On the day, there were information stands providing up-to-date information on learning opportunities locally and nationally, which gave people the opportunity to speak to specialists, find out about training and most importantly, develop confidence in trying new things. The event also included a number of workshops on study skills, creative writing, access to funding and older people as tutors.	Opportunities New things Confidence

Reduce to
Key words

Use the words to
construct a pattern

Sum up in sentences
or phrases

Figure 3.1 How to move to pattern notes from reading

● **Tips:**
● Move to keyword notes in stages –see page 76.
● For a pattern note of this advice – see page 79.
● For an example of a student's notes on reading Tony Buzan – see page 81.

Notes, sources and plagiarism

▨ **Sources:** When making notes from your reading always put the source in your notes. You have to give this information in the Bibliography that you must compile at the end of your essay. Record the information in the way that your tutor wants:

▨ **Harvard System:** Author, date (of publication), *Title* (or 'title' if a journal article), publisher, town of publication.

▨ **British Standard System:** Author, *Title* (Or 'Title'), publisher, date of publication.

▨ **Quotes:** If you copy sections of the text into your notes to use as quotes put the page numbers in your notes. When you quote in your writing you must give author, date and page number.

▨ **Building a permanent record:** Start an index card collection of all your reading. Buy an index box and alphabet dividers. Each time you read record author, date, title, and publisher on an index card. Write a brief description of the text – record a few key points. File alphabetically. In this way you will build a huge record of all your reading: a fabulous resource in itself.

▨ **Plagiarism:** Plagiarism means kidnapping – and if you do not give your sources when you write you are in effect kidnapping someone else's work and passing it off as your own. Plagiarism is a major academic offence which can get you a fail for a module – or even lose you your whole degree.

▨ **'Well, I read it, I agreed with it and now I've put it in my own words – it's mine now. I don't have to give sources then, do I?'** Yes you do – the ideas still came from someone else. And anyway, you are supposed to be giving sources – you are not supposed to be making it all up!

▨ **'How many sources should I give then?'** As a rule of thumb, a first year degree essay should have between eight and 15 items listed in the bibliography. It goes upwards from there.

R is for Review

The final part of the QOOQRRR strategy is the **review**. This is where you should look over your own notes and judge for yourself whether or not they are useful, useable and suited to your purpose. Remember that the goal is for you to become an active learner in control of your own learning. It is up to you to decide whether or not your notes are any good. But there are some things to look out for when you are judging your own notes.

Note review questions:

1 **Are your notes sourced?** That is, have you recorded author, date, *Title*, publisher, town? Have you noted page numbers besides quotes?

2 **Have you copied quotes out accurately?** When quoting you must get it exactly right. You can abbreviate a quote – but then you must put in an ellipsis (dot, dot, dot …) to show where you made the cut. You can change a word, but then you must put square brackets [ ] around the word that you have changed in the quote.

3 **Do your notes do what you wanted them to?** That is, if you needed a few quotes for a piece of writing – do you have them? Are they sourced? If you needed to gain the overview of a topic – have you?

4 **Scan!** If anything is missing from your notes – scan the piece again to find the missing bits of information. (Scanning is one of those skills that you bring with you to academic reading – it is the same as when you programme a telephone number into your brain, run a finger down the page of the directory and lo and behold the number just jumps out at you.)

5 **Is there anything else that I ought to read now?** Many texts will mention other people (often as their own evidence): you can read what these people have written. There will also be other books on your reading list and journal articles to read. Once you have read one thing you have to decide what if anything you should now read – and when. Get out your calendar and see if you have time for it – make a date, for if you do not set a date it will not get done.

6 **Do I stop reading now?** At some point your reading has to stop. Yes, you must read widely, but beware – do not use your reading as an excuse to put off writing – it is something that we are all tempted to do at one time or another.

When you are happy with your notes you are ready to move on to your next task.

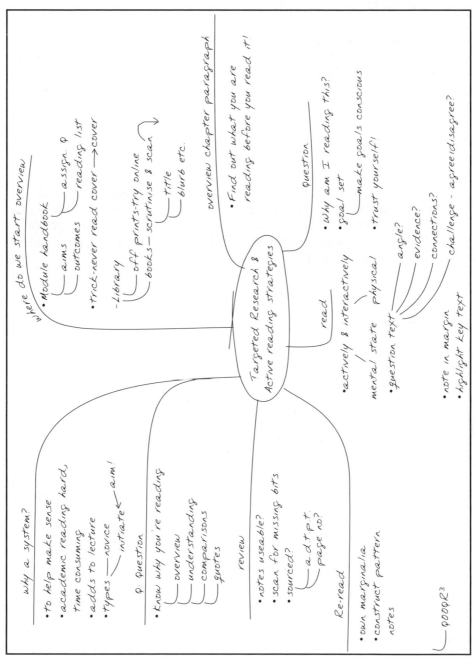

Figure 3.2 Pattern notes on QOOQRRR

Conclusion

We have covered research and reading with a special focus on becoming an active reader of academic texts. We have also spent some considerable time on the QOOQRRR technique. In the process we outlined the strategy that has proven the most useful with our students. We have emphasised the need for active question, overview, overview, question, read, re-read and review strategies – these will necessitate you becoming active and interactive when reading and will work towards increasing your understanding as you develop and use critical and analytical skills as you read.

We have mentioned that some people do find academic reading frightening, and that some also find even the notion of developing an effective reading strategy really intimidating. We did not do this to intimidate you but rather to offer reassurance. If any of these fears are true for you – they will pass. As always we recommend practise, practise, practise as the way of moving forward.

Keep it up

- Continue through this book using these QOOQRRR techniques.

- Question: when reading look back at your learning contract – what one thing are you looking for?

- Overview: remember your overview of the book – what are you reading?

- Overview: with each chapter, get the overview by looking at the introduction and conclusion. Jot down what the chapter is about.

- Question: set your own goals for a specific chapter: Why am I reading this? What do I want? What do I need? Where will I use the information? How will I know when I have what I want?

- Read: actively and interactively – marking up useful sections as you go.

- Re-read: your own notes – use those to construct your key word notes.

- Review your own notes – judge whether or not they are helpful.

- Review again: review the QOOQRRR system and see how it works for you.

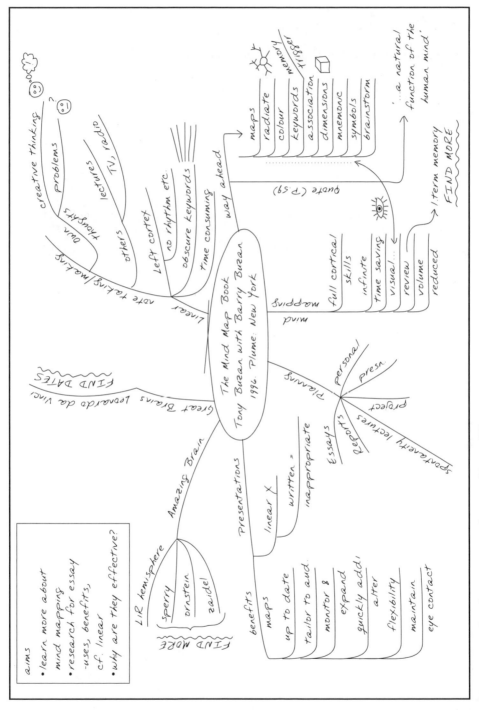

Figure 3.3 Student notes on her reading of Buzan

Review points

When you reflect on this chapter you might notice that you have:

- [ ] considered the nature of research – including primary and secondary sources

- [ ] realised the importance of reading for the student

- [ ] started the process of reading effectively

- [ ] gained an understanding of targeted research and active reading strategies (QOOQRRR)

- [ ] engaged with various activities that have reinforced your understanding of the different parts of the chapter.

4 How to use the overview (the big picture)

Aims

To introduce you to the importance of gaining an overview of any course that you join. (In Chapter 5 we will link the 'overview' to an exploration of memory, learning style, revision and exam techniques.)

Learning outcomes

That after reading this chapter and engaging with the activities, you will have:

- considered the importance of the overview
- an understanding of how to gain an overview of a course
- considered how having an overview of a course will assist your active learning
- put overview theory into practice with respect to this book.

Introduction

In this chapter we will be examining how the active learner can take control of a course from the moment that they join it. We will pay close attention to the need for gaining an overview of the course – and we will explain how the overview helps you to prepare for course assessment. We will look at how courses are usually put together in colleges and universities in England and Wales.

Activity: Goal setting

As always – before you progress through the chapter, pause and reflect quickly on the chapter topics, ask yourself:

■ What do I already know on these topics?

■ What would I like to know?

Once you have brainstormed and set your own goals, you are ready to move on as an active learner.

Big picture: the importance of the overview

The overview is essential for the active learner and this is what this chapter is all about (see Chapter 3 to see how an overview assists with academic reading). Further we believe that it will also help you as a student if you understand how courses are put together: we will explore how courses are typically put together in England and Wales – and we will highlight this by taking you through some suggested aims and learning outcomes for this book. We will close this section by considering how detailed understanding of the overview can directly help with an assessment.

Don't be a passenger

Whenever we start a school, college or university course we join a programme that has been designed and planned by other people. Even though we are not necessarily aware that this is the case, it can have a negative effect on us as students. We can get the sense that the course 'belongs' to other people – not to us.

A negative consequence of this is that it can make us passive receivers of a course rather than active negotiators of that course. The passive receiver might just drift through the course in a bit of a daze. Because the course belongs to someone else, they just bob along on top of it. Moving from week to week maybe accepting what is going on – maybe not; but not actively engaging with the course.

Obviously you cannot get the most from a course – or from yourself as a student – if you approach your studies in this way. In this book we continually stress the importance of active, interactive learning and of you, the student, becoming an active learner – an active student in control of your own learning. So how can you make this happen?

So get the overview

A simple way of starting off the process of taking control of a particular course is to gain an overview of that course. Then you can use the overview to help you understand the shape, direction and make up of the course – and to then take control of the course itself – and of your own learning of the information in that course. This process is sometimes called 'owning your own learning'.

A very simple analogy is that a course can be compared to a jigsaw puzzle that is being put together week by week. It is much easier to put the puzzle together if we have the big picture (the overview) in front of us as we go along. And it is much easier to actively engage with a course of study if you have the big picture of the course before you start to try to piece all the different bits of information together in a way that makes sense of the whole course. Before we move on to discuss how to gain an overview of a course, we will quickly examine how formal programmes of study are typically shaped by institutions and tutors.

How courses are put together in England and Wales

In colleges

GNVQ, **AS** and **A2** courses in school or college are typically designed and managed by external examining bodies. These shape the courses and design the assessment strategies. Individual institutions sign up to particular examining bodies and their programmes.

Course tutors are supplied with information on the aims, outcomes and assessment strategies of the course. Each tutor then has to design their teaching weeks (the syllabus) to help students learn sufficient material to get them to pass that course. Typically some mixture of course work and exams assess each course, of these the exams are set and marked externally.

Many tutors will put together a course handbook of some sort that will reveal to students what it is that they are supposed to be learning. Often this is expressed as the aims and learning outcomes.

● **Tips:**
● Many GNVQ, AS and A2 courses are serviced by extensive on-line resources. It is in your interest to check these out.
● Aims and outcomes for these programmes may be very wordy. If these are not helpful, pay especial attention to past exam papers for these will tell you quite simply what is on a typical exam paper – and hence they tell you what you will need to know to pass the course.

Access programmes are slightly different to GNVQ and A level courses. Tutors can get 'off the shelf' units or modules from an access validating body – or they can design their own courses which they then have validated by such a body.

If tutors design their own programmes, the aims, outcomes and assessment criteria will all be closely scrutinised by the validating body. The learning outcomes must all be demonstrably tested via specific assessment criteria for the course to be validated. That is, every learning outcome that a tutor writes up must have an assessment criterion attached to it. Tutors are not allowed to describe a learning outcome that is not assessed.

The validating body will also supply Access programmes with external moderators whose job it is to check that the course is running as it should be and that standards as set out in the course documentation are being met. That is, the moderators will check assessment criteria against learning outcomes – and that these are being marked by the course tutors.

● **Tip:** Access students should check that they meet **all** the assessment criteria in a specific piece of work. They will need to meet all the assessment criteria to receive credits at the required level.

At university

University tutors often design their own courses – a university committee including external examiners then validates these. When tutors plan courses they have to work out what the 'learning outcomes' for that course are. As with all the above examples, these learning outcomes are the things that the student has to learn as they work through the taught sessions – lectures, tutorials, and seminars – and other activities – reading and assignments.

As with the above, the learning outcomes have to be tested; that is, the student is assessed as to whether or not they have achieved those learning outcomes. Hence, the assessments, whatever they are, are designed to test whether or not the learning outcomes have been met.

Typically once the assessments are collected in, a course tutor marks all student work. A sample will be double marked. A selection will be sent to an external examiner who will be checking that marks are awarded appropriately and against learning outcomes.

● **Tip:** Know the learning outcomes for a course and you know what you will be tested on.

How to gain an overview of a course

Whether you are a college or a university student the easiest way to gain an overview of a course is to discover its learning outcomes. They give the big picture; once you have that, you can work out the small steps that you would have to take to get to the end of the course – and to pass it. (Hence the sub-title of the 'how to pass exams' chapter: big picture – small steps.)

Many college and university course tutors produce course booklets or module handbooks that reveal the learning outcomes quite explicitly. If they do not do so, there maybe on-line materials that might help. Failing that, college or university students might have to use past exam papers as their sole source of information as to where the course is going, what is to be assessed – and how it is to be assessed.

Get the overview

Once you join a particular course of study there are several really useful things to do immediately to gain an overview of the course:

- **Course booklet/module handbook.** If your tutor has prepared a booklet or handbook to support the course that you are on, make sure that you have a copy. Once you have a copy – read it!

- **Aims and outcomes.** Many course booklets or handbooks spell out the overall aims of the programme as well as the specific learning outcomes. (You might have noticed by now that we also do this at the beginning of each chapter of this book.) Your first task as a student would be to explore the course booklet or handbook to see what the aims and outcomes tell you about the course.

● **Tip:** Highlight key words – make notes or a list. Pin this list up in your study space to help keep you focused on the goals of the course. Look at the learning outcome key words when preparing for a class, your reading and an assignment.

- **Assessment.** Once you have analysed the aims and outcomes, move on to examine the way the course is going to be assessed. The course may be 100% course work, 100% exam-based or some mixture of the two. Course work typically involves the production of one or more of the following: essay, report, write-up of a practical, presentation, etc. Exams can be just as varied: seen or unseen paper (with the former you receive the exam paper in advance of the exam itself, with the latter you receive the paper at the beginning of the exam proper). Exams can be one, two or three hours in length. They might involve you writing essay answers, short answers or responding to multiple choice questions. Exams may be 'open book'; here you can take certain books into the examination room.

● **Tip:** In assessments you must answer the questions but you must also meet the learning outcomes!

- **Read the question(s).** Often course work questions (assignments) are given at the beginning of the course, in the handbook. Read the question! You are not expected to know the answer yet – but if you read the question you will know what the course is designed to get you to be able to answer.

● **Tip:** Write out the question. Underline the key words. Pin the question on your wall. Read up around one word at a time (using QOOQRRR – Chapter 3); listen for information on the key words in lectures and classes.

■ **Look at past papers.** If there is an exam component to your course, find past exam papers and read them. As with the course work assignment, these tell you what you should be able to answer by the end of the course. They help you to set your learning goals for the course.

● **Tip:** Don't forget to add any relevant information to the whole batch of timetables that you were advised to draw up in Chapter 2!

■ **Examine the syllabus.** Sometimes we are lucky and we are given a week by week programme for the course that we are on – this is sometimes called the timetable, syllabus or scheme of work. Read it. Have a look at how the course has been put together. Notice which weeks are designed to cover which learning outcomes.

● **Tip:** Colour-code your learning outcomes – you can then also colour code your syllabus.

Now let us go through the various processes recommended above with respect to this very book.

Activity: Putting 'overview' theory into practice by gaining an overview of this book

Essential Study Skills

Aims

The aims of this Study Skills book are to introduce you to a range of skills, techniques and strategies that are designed to facilitate effective study.

Learning outcomes

By the end of engaging with this book it is hoped that you will:

1 Have considered the study and academic skills and practices necessary for effective study.

2 Have practised the various study and academic skills and practices covered in this book.

▶

3 Have reflected on your use of the various study and academic skills and practices so that you can select relevant skills and practices at appropriate times in your study (for example notemaking skills, research and reading strategies, effective communication practices).

4 Have reflected on the overall practices of successful study so that you have started the process of becoming a more effective student.

Comment: What do you think about these aims and outcomes?

Hopefully, the above aims and outcomes are clear and logical, but more than that, they should tell you what the book is designed to **do** – and hence what you could get out of the book. This allows you to set your own goals as you work through the book.

● **Tip:** If you have not already done so, now might be the time to fill in a learning contract for this book. Try answering the following questions:

1 What do I want from this book?

2 What am I prepared to do to achieve my goals?

3 What might stop me?

4 What's in it for me?

There's more – learning outcomes help with assignments

The learning outcomes should also inform you that any assessment activity based on this book would have to be designed to test that you had met **all** of the above learning outcomes.

So in any particular assignment attached to this book you would have to demonstrate that you had:

■ Considered the skills and practices. That is, read and thought about them.

■ Practised the skills. That is, done something with them. Ideally you should have used one or more of the skills and practices covered in this book.

■ Reflected on your use of those skills and practices. That is, once you had used the skill, you would be expected to think about your use of that skill. As this is a practical book designed to help you develop those skills, your use of the skill might tell you how much more practice you think you would have put in to become more confident with the skill. You might also reflect on how you would continue to use the skill and how valuable it is to you as a student.

■ Started the process of becoming a more effective student. That is, have some sort of overall comment to make about yourself as an effective student. And that conclusion would be based on the above – that is, your knowledge of, use of and reflection on particular skills and practices.

Query: Can you now see that once you know the learning outcomes it should be very difficult to get a course 'wrong'?

Do all learning outcomes help?

Maybe not all learning outcomes will be as easy to translate into specific assignment requirements as others. But the overall principle is always the same. Further, the more practice you get at reading learning outcomes and comparing them with assessment questions and criteria, the better you will get at making and using the links between the two.

● **Tips**
If you are ever in doubt with your learning outcomes, there are several things you can do:
● Work through the learning outcomes and assessment criteria with your study partner.
● Ask the course tutor to help you make sense of the outcomes and criteria.
● Ask the learning development people at your college or university for help with this technique.

Conclusion

In this section we have looked at the importance of gaining the overview of any course that we study. We have called this the gaining of the 'big picture'. Further we argued that gaining the big picture allows you to make sense of and understand a course and hence helps you to become an active learner on that course.

Once you have a sense of what a course is trying to do, you can take control of your own learning and navigate your way rather than being a mere passenger on that course.

We moved on to explore how different courses are put together – and to see how in each case the learning outcomes work to define the assessments. We made it clear that knowing the learning outcomes of a course helps you to prepare for the assessment.

Review points

When reviewing this chapter you might realise that you now have:

☐ an understanding of the role of the overview with respect to active learning

☐ a sense of what the overview (especially aims and outcomes) tells you about the direction of a course

☐ an understanding of how the overview will tell you what you need to do and learn to pass a particular course

☐ an understanding of how the overview can directly assist with assessment preparation.

5 How to pass exams (big picture – small steps)

Aims

To explore exams, memory, learning style, revision and exam techniques such that you will be able to succeed in your exams.

Learning outcomes

That after reading this chapter and engaging with the activities, you will have:

■ considered the nature of exams – and some responses to exams

■ linked overview theory to exam success (big picture – small steps)

■ considered the difference between short and long term memory

■ considered different learning styles and made decisions about your own learning strategies

■ been introduced to a whole course approach to exam success

■ been introduced to successful learning, revision and exam strategies.

Introduction

The subtitle for this chapter is 'big picture – small steps'. We wanted to indicate that whilst a course does have a big picture – an overall shape, purpose and direction – we generally then make sense of (and learn) a course one piece at a time: we take small steps through the course.

In this section we are going to explore how the big picture allows you to take small steps to learning course content and ultimately passing exams. In the process of doing this we will examine memory, learning style, revision and exam techniques. We will start this off with a quick look at typical responses to exams.

Activity: Goal setting

As always, before you progress through the chapter, pause and reflect quickly on the chapter topics, ask yourself:

■ What do I already know on these topics?

■ What would I like to know?

■ What do I like about my memory at the moment?

■ What do I want to improve?

■ What do I like about my revision and exam techniques?

■ What would I like to improve?

Once you have brainstormed and set your own goals, you are ready to move on as an active learner.

Small steps: preparing for exams

Whilst some aspects of studying will always fill some students with horror, examinations (exams) are loathed by most people. We believe that this situation arises because of early schooling experiences – and early exam experiences. We are going to explore some reasons why students may not like exams, we will move on to consider memory and learning style. Finally we shall give very specific and practical advice entitled SQP4 – a whole course approach to passing exams.

So, what's wrong with exams?

Firstly the problem is not necessarily with exams at all, but often lies in approaches to teaching and learning, and in how we are taught, at school, college and even in universities. That is, whilst we are taught subject content we are not necessarily taught how to learn that content.

Some teachers believe that just presenting students with information will guarantee that those students will pass the exams. But presentation is not learning. It is good to know what we ought to learn – but in the end the student has to somehow learn the material for him or herself if they want to use that information successfully to pass an exam. For it is the student that has to pass the exam, not the tutor.

So how do we learn course material?

Carl Rogers, psychologist and teacher, believed that what the tutor has to do is facilitate significant learning in the student. That is, the tutor has to set up a learning situation, but the student has to then actively decide to learn. He described this process as the student reaching out for what they want and need. Most of the activities in this book are designed to help you, the student, reach out for what you want and need – initially from this very book itself and then from all your studies. But in this section we will be specifically focusing on how to learn course material in order that you do pass your exams.

'Why haven't we done this before?'

It can be really frustrating for students to turn up at university and realise that they have to take all the responsibility for their own learning – when they have not actually been taught how to do this. This can be especially galling when it comes to passing university exams. The grades that they get in their exams will determine what class of degree they receive – and typically they do really want to do well but they do not know how to do well. If this is how you feel, then you know what we mean!

I'd be fine if it wasn't for the exams

Often the most motivated student still does not know how to do well in exams. Naturally enough, this guarantees that the majority of people never perform very well in their exams. Thus a vicious circle of unpreparedness and exam failure sets in. Eventually many people just give up on exams. These people tend to think that the problem lies with them – they are not clever enough, they are not suited to exams… whatever. The reality is that they have often not been taught how to learn or how to approach exams.

Exams are simply misunderstood

The nature of how we prepare for exams, or not, leads to the second point about exams – they are often misunderstood. Many people have criticised exams for the high failure rates in this country, for not being educationally sound, for being set in hay fever season, for disadvantaging people with high stress levels and so forth. But it could be argued that what these people are doing is attacking the symptom – the high failure rates in exams – rather than the problem – that we do not teach people how to learn.

For there is a sound educational purpose to exams. Exams are designed not just to test your memory of key facts and data, your surface learning. (Though remember that these are often very important, too.) Exams are there to test your deep learning, your knowledge and under-standing of material. That is, to test how you use the information that you have learned – and that you have made your own through reorgani-sation and understanding – over a whole course of study.

If we refer back to our earlier points on learning, that it is about being able to:

■ gather

■ record

■ organise

■ understand

■ remember, and

■ use...information.

Then perhaps you can see that exams are designed to force you to demonstrate that you have indeed learned your material so that you can flexibly use the information again in an examination. Yes – this does all occur in a time controlled situation and this can feel very stressful, but the overall idea is not to trick you, but to test you. If you can accept that, then you are on your way to dealing more positively with the exam situation.

Further, some people do actually enjoy the idea of being tested, finding it a challenge. So if you really, really hate exams at the moment – work on changing your attitude. Try to see exams as a challenge, an opportunity to demonstrate what you do know, rather than a problem. It really will help you, if you could look at exams in a more positive light.

It's a trick

Many people are so stressed by the idea of exams that they can only see the negative aspects. Exams feel like trickery – evil things designed to catch you out. Fear means that it is difficult to see that the exam is a test, not a trick. It is often fear itself that prevents these people from preparing for exams. Even if they do prepare – fear can have such a negative effect on the brain (release of the stress hormones cortisol and adrenalin which reduce short-term memory) that they cannot remember what they are trying to learn.

If this describes how you feel about exams, you really will have to change your basic negative approach before you will be able to move forward.

● **Tips**
● Have a look at material on positive thinking – see Chapter 7 to start you off.
● Understand that exams are a test, not a trick.
● Work towards particular exams with a study partner.
● Use the learning development (sometimes caused learning support, study skills or study development) people at your college or university to help you prepare for exams.
● Use the counselling service to help you get over your fear of exams.

I'm dyslexic and I write really slowly

Many students ask us how long an exam answer should be. What can we tell them? There really is no right or wrong answer because in the end there is only what you can write in the time you have been allowed. So every student has to discover how much they can write (how many words) in the time allowed – and then get better at answering an exam question in that many words.

This problem can be exacerbated for the dyslexic student who probably writes more slowly than most. However, there are still some positive things that you can do. First, if you think that you are dyslexic, you must get a proper test done. Go to the Student Support Services at your college or university to find out how this happens.

You can then use the test results to lobby for extra time in exams. Typically the dyslexic student is allowed another ten minutes per hour in an exam. This does have some value. However, if you also lobby to take exams on a word processor or computer, this can have a marked effect on your grades. Students we know who have done this have turned the exam situation around dramatically – moving from an automatic fail in exams to gaining upper second and even first grades.

There are several reasons why this could be the case:

■ word-processed work looks so much neater, it overcomes any unconscious prejudice in the mind of the examiner towards untidy handwriting

■ the student feels so much more confident on the computer that they do indeed produce better work

■ the student actually practises more.

Tips
● Practise timed writing.
● Practise answering assignment questions, but where you would normally be allowed upwards of 1,500 words, give yourself half an hour.
● Practise preparing perfect answers with your study partner.
● If using a computer – learn to touch type.
● Practise timed writing on the computer.

How can you learn a whole year's work in three weeks?

Contrary to popular opinion, revision is **not** something that you should be doing just before your exams. As we are constantly reiterating here, revision is part of active learning. You should be learning material as you go through your course – not just before the exams. What you do just before the exams is practise that timed writing.

● **Tip:** Read the section on SQP4 – this will give a whole course approach to passing exams.

But I've got a really bad memory

Many people feel that they have a bad memory, often this is because they have not actually learned how to use their memories (they have not learned how to learn). There is also the argument that, especially as we get older, we focus more on what we are forgetting, instead of noticing what we are remembering.

Everyone can develop a good memory. London cab drivers, for example, have measurably larger cortexes to their brains because they have had to teach themselves to remember all the streets, alleys and roads in London. What the London cabby can do, you can do! The trick is to learn how to remember.

Tips
● Check out the section below on memory.
● Get the overview of the course.
● Check out the learning outcomes.
● Learn key points on any course as you go.

Memory and learning style

This whole book is dedicated to active learning. If you put active learning techniques into practice – you will learn. This is especially so if you **want** to learn specific material (hence our stress on the learning contract). Here we are going to actively tackle issues around memory. We will then move on to look at how information about learning style can also help you to learn more effectively.

So, do you think that you have a good memory? Whenever we ask that question of a group of students, the majority always responds that they have a bad memory. However, there is an argument that everyone can develop a good memory – with practice.

Memory

Tony Buzan has explored the psychology and dynamics of memory with respect to learning. His work on remembering and forgetting curves has led him to argue that we need to actively revise (learn) everything that we want to remember. He states that, without active revision, we forget 98% of what we encounter after just three weeks. This means that if we do not act to remember what we want to remember (our course work) – we forget it **all**.

This is obviously a real problem for those who revise only three weeks before an exam. For what these people are doing is not revision – it is learning it all from scratch. And no, you cannot do that in three weeks.

The revision cycle

Buzan recommends an active revision cycle when encountering new and important material:

1 The same day that you encountered the new material, spend ten minutes making a short, dynamic version of your notes. Build in memory triggers. Memory triggers might be cartoons or illustrations that make a particular page of notes easier to remember for you.

2 A day later spend two minutes recalling your memory trigger – and the notes attached. You might mentally recall the information or actually re-draw the notes. The more active you are the better.

3 A week later spend another two minutes reactivating the memory.

4 A month later spend another two minutes reactivating the memory.

5 Reactivate every six months for as long as you want to keep the memory alive.

You can see that the revision cycle is a sort of 'use it or lose it' cycle. It is a system based on transferring information from our relatively ineffectual short-term memories into our infinitely more useful long-term memories. In the process of doing this we are actually building memories chemically into our brains.

Short- and long-term memory

Buzan's research adds to what is believed about our short- and long-term memories (see Figure 5.1). The belief is that the short-term memory is a very small and immediate working memory. This allows us to function day-to-day. However, our long-term memories are memories that we create and build. It could be argued that these allow us to function in our lives – they become who we are. In terms of our studying, the short-term memory is good for picking up pieces of information – but we need to get that information into our long-term memories if it is to be of any use to us.

Getting information into our long-term memories does not happen by accident or chance. It does not happen quickly – but over time. It does not happen unless **we** do something to make it happen. Basically if we do want to learn something, then we have to:

■ choose what to remember

■ decide how we are going to remember it (our memory triggers)

■ be prepared to reactivate the memory immediately, then a day, a week and a month later (use the revision cycle)

■ make yet another commitment of time and effort to our studies.

Activity: Think back to how you learned things in primary school or kindergarten

Spend five minutes jotting down how you learned things in your earliest days at school.

Now compare your list with points taken from other students:

- I learned the alphabet by singing a little alphabet song. It is still the way I remember the alphabet.

- We were taught our sums by reciting the times tables. But I don't actually remember them now. I don't think I wanted to learn my tables – so that didn't work so well.

- I remember the colours of the rainbow, you know: Richard of York Gained Battle In Vain. If you take the first letters you can get back to Red, Orange, Yellow, Green, Blue, Indigo, Violet.

- One that my little girl came home with the other day was the spelling of 'because' – **b**ig **e**lephants **c**an **a**lways **u**nderstand **s**mall **e**lephants.

- And then there is that other one – Never Eat Shredded Wheat – which gives you the points of the compass… North, East, South, West.

Query: How do these memory systems compare with the ones that you have noted down?

Discussion: What is actually happening here is that the teacher, typically, is designing mnemonics (memory systems or triggers) for the students. Where the trigger involves rhythm and rhyme (the alphabet song) – and the student wants to remember – it seems to be more successful. Where the trigger involves something unusual or bizarre (Richard of York – or the big elephants) it is also more memorable.

We put aside childish things

Unfortunately, what seems to happen as we get older is that we stop using these successful memory strategies, strategies that seem to work with the way that our brains actually work. It seems that as we grow to be adults, instead of becoming more proficient learners we put aside successful learning strategies, it is as if we deliberately forget how to learn! What we need to do now is to relearn how to learn. When we apply that to our studies, we will have to work out what it is that we want to remember – and then decide how we are going to remember it – using the systems that work with our brains.

● **Tips**
● Design your own mnemonic systems for all the things that you need to remember.
● Use rhythm and rhyme.
● Use the bizarre.
● Reduce key information onto index cards, carry them about and revise in odd moments.

Short-term memory	Attribute	Long-term memory
Relatively small – holds 5–9 pieces of information	Capacity – size	Infinite – can build an infinite number of memories in the brain
Brief – piece of information number 8 comes along – and a piece of information falls out	Persistence – how long information stays	Infinite – with reactivation and barring brain trauma – information can stay there forever
Is immediate – either it goes in or it does not	Input – how to get information in	Relatively slow – see revision cycle. It takes time and effort to build memories
Is immediate – if it is there you can access it	Access – how to get information out	Depends on input. How you put it in is how you get it out (alphabet song)

Figure 5.1 The main attributes of short- and long-term memory

Learning style

In the section on memory, above, we asked you to think back to your experiences at primary school in order to recall how you used to remember. If you went to a Montessori primary school, you would perhaps have noticed that you were actually encouraged to see, hear, say and do everything. This is because we learn a proportion of what we see or hear or say or do – but the argument is that we learn 90% of what we see, hear, say **and** do.

A branch of psychology entitled NLP (neuro-linguistic programming) developed this into an exploration of primary, secondary and tertiary learning pathways – and they then linked learning pathway to learning style. They argue that we all favour either visual (sight based), auditory (sound based) or kinaesthetic (touch, feel or movement based) learning styles. To encourage personal learning, we should favour our personal learning style; but to guarantee complete learning we should utilise all the learning pathways – hence the success of see, hear, say and do techniques.

Activity: What's my learning style?

One way to check your primary learning pathway is to examine the language that you use. For example, are you be the sort of person who says:

- I see what you mean? or

- I hear what you're saying? or

- It feels good to me?

'I see what you mean' indicates that you use sight-based language, and you might favour the visual learning pathway.

'I hear what you're saying' indicates that you could favour an auditory pathway (hear and say).

'It feels good to me' possibly indicates that you are a kinaesthetic type person (touch, feel, movement).

Still not sure? Well, if remembering a spelling would you:

- See the word in your mind, possibly write it down, and see if it looks right? (Visual)

- Sound out the letters and hear if it sounds right? (Auditory)

- Look at or say the word – but check if it feels right? (Kinaesthetic)

● **Tips**
● **Sight:** if you remember mainly by sight, you may enjoy learning by reading and watching television, film or video. You could use pictures in your learning and revision activities: draw pattern notes, put in colour, and put in memory jogging cartoon images or visuals.
● **Sound:** if you remember sounds best, you may enjoy learning through listening and joining in discussions or explaining things to other people. You could benefit from using audio-tapes to support your learning and you could use songs, rhymes and jingles that you write yourself as learning and revision aids. Tape yourself and sing along.
● **Feel:** if you remember the feel of things, you may enjoy practical learning activities from making something, to performing a science experiment to role-playing. Making charts and patterns of the things you want to remember will help your learning and revision – as will acting out in some way.

Key words, key facts

In Chapter 6 on creative learning we will be talking about pattern notes. This is a key-word notemaking system that utilises visual techniques – pattern, colour, and cartoons – to assist learning. The visual aspects are important and build on what we know about learning style – but another thing that we emphasise is the importance of **key word** notes. We continually stress that you the student should reduce chunks of information to the key words that could be used to sum up or stand for that information.

Indeed a key to successful learning is not to try to remember whole chunks of texts. It really is not an advantage to try for word for word recall of whole lectures or seminars, of whole essays that you or other students have written or of whole passages from books; this can be really ineffective. This is inefficient because it is passive, because basically you would be remembering too much padding along with the information – and because it can actually stop you from being able to use the information yourself.

To be both active and effective in our learning we have to develop our ability to strip back what we need to learn to the bare essentials. Once we have learned key data, we need to be able to **use** it ourselves. We need to be able to use our key data in discussion, in presentations and in our writing – including our exam writing. If we simply remember how other people have used the information – in lectures or in textbooks, for example – we can become trapped into those ways ourselves.

Add flesh to the bones – later

So the trick is to reduce information to its bare essentials – which we do then learn by heart – and then to practise using the information for ourselves. This is especially important as we move through a course towards the exams. Week by week we can reduce our notes to ever fewer words that we know very deeply – and that we use constantly (more on this below in SQP4). Thus we reduce the quantity of what we have to learn (the amount) but improve the quality (we can use it ourselves, with confidence).

As you reduce information to the bare essentials you can utilise 'see, hear, say and do' strategies to ensure that you are going to remember the maximum amount of that information. That is, you can use the information on learning styles to develop your revision strategies.

Using your learning style

Use your learning style to learn your key words:

See
If you are visual, you may enjoy learning by reading and using visual aids (television, film or video). It would help if you made revision notes as colourful as possible – and visual triggers would definitely help you to remember.

Hear/say

If you prefer an auditory learning style, then lectures, discussion and audio-tapes would all help you to learn. For revision purposes, it would help if you put your key word data into jingles or songs – or if you used funny voices when revising.

Feel/do

If you favour a kinaesthetic learning approach you will benefit from building a physical dimension into your learning – this could be really simple, like moving about as you study (very different, though from the notion of the good student sitting quietly in one place for hours on end!). Your learning and revision would benefit from **making** your pattern notes – perhaps cutting out memory triggers from magazines and physically pasting them onto your notes.

Activity: Have some fun!

A good tip with respect to learning material is to make a game of it – to inject some fun into the proceedings! Designing revision games for programmes really helps learning.

Activity: If you had to design a revision game for one of your programmes of study, what would you do? (Think for five minutes – then compare your ideas with those below.)

Typically students have designed:

- Quizzes – here the students researched a specific programme (sociology, psychology, history) etc. examining the aims and learning outcomes. Once they identified the key data (names, dates, information) that ought to be learned by the end of the course, they designed questions and answers that covered all the ground on that course. A competitive edge was set up for the quiz by having several teams competing against each other. Answering the questions or not revealed to the players both the information they had learned – and that which they had forgotten.

- Board games – here again, the students researched a programme examining the aims and learning outcomes. They again constructed questions and answers that covered all the learning outcomes (the key data – names, dates, and information). But here they designed a colourful board game that could be played as the questions were answered.

Discussion: Both these strategies are very effective with respect to learning the key information on a course.

▶

The quiz utilises 'see, hear and say' strategies, and the playing of the quiz can become an emotional and even a physical experience.

The board game scenario is especially good, for to play the game you will see, hear, say and do!

Activity: Learning style revision games

Choose one section of this book. Reduce the information to key word points. Design a revision game that would help you learn the material. Play the game with your study partner.

SQP4: putting it all together – a practical guide

In this section we will bring all the information about the use of the overview, memory and learning style together into our very practical revision and exam technique advice – **SQP4: survey, question, predict, plan, prepare and practise**. We will close with a look at 'examination day'.

Activity: Thinking about exams

Some people are so frightened of exams that they do not prepare for them at all – is this you? Obviously we believe this is a bad idea: if you never prepare, you will probably always do quite badly and this could keep you feeling bad about exams for the rest of your life. So let us compare exams to other things that you might choose to do. Compare exams to:

- running a marathon
- passing a driving test
- entering a dance competition.

Choose one of these and think how you would prepare for it. (5 minutes)

Now compare your answer with that given by a student below:

'When planning for my driving test I sorted out the written test first. I got the book with the key questions in and tested myself till I thought I'd got them right.

▶

Then I got my friends to test me till I was sure I'd got it right. I only lost two points in the test itself.

'With the driving part, I had lessons till my instructor thought I was ready. When I was confident that I knew how to do it, I booked the test. Then my instructor and I practised all the things that would definitely come up in the test – you know emergency stop, three-point turn, and parking properly.

When I could drive a car in my sleep – I took the test and passed first time.'

Discussion: When it comes to the sorts of 'test' that we choose to do in our everyday life, we do know what to do. We:

■ **find out** exactly what will be required of us in the test

■ **learn** the things that we need to learn

■ **practise often.**

That is the essence of the SQP4 system.

Survey

As soon as you start on a course, get the overview of the course as a whole (see Chapter 4). This is the big picture part of your whole course approach to exam success.

■ If you have a course booklet or handbook, check the aims and learning outcomes. Make key word notes summarising all the things that will be assessed.

■ If supplied with a syllabus, read it through and note which weeks are dedicated to which of the learning outcomes and mark them up. See how many weeks are set to cover each topic and use that to try and gain a sense of how important each thing is.

■ Read the assignment question for more information on what to do and learn on the course. Further, this reveals the sorts of questions that you could be asked on the course itself. Cross-reference the different parts of the assignment question with different weeks on the course. This helps you to take control of course content and delivery.

■ Look for past exam papers to see exactly the style of the paper. Discover how long the exam will be, how many questions you will be expected to answer and the sorts of topics that come up all the time. Notice the way questions are written on an exam paper so that the real paper cannot frighten you!

Where are my papers?

Sometimes past papers are actually given to students, sometimes they are not. When they are not, you have to discover where they are kept.

With national exams taken by college students, past papers are sometimes kept in the college library. Sample papers may be kept on the on-line website designed to support the course.

Universities operate many different systems for storing exam papers – even across a single university. Some departments put papers on-line, some hold them in the university library, and others place them with the departmental secretary. It is your task both to find out where they are kept – and to actually have a good look at them. Photocopy the papers and put them into your subject file!

● **Tip:** Write an 'exam' list for each course that you are taking, note:
  how long the exam will be
  how many questions you will have to answer
  whether it is a seen or unseen exam (where you get the paper in advance)
  whether or not it is an open book exam (whether or not you will be
  allowed to take text books into the exam).

Question

Once you have spent real time surveying the course to gain your overview, you are ready to move on to Q for question. That is, very early on in a course you need to reflect on all the information that you have gathered from your overview – your active surveying of the course. You need to sit down and ask yourself – **what exactly do I need to do and learn to pass this course?**

Make a list of all the things that you will need to do and learn to pass the course – pin it up in your study space. Do this for every course or module or unit that you are taking.

● **Tips**
● Draw up your lists with your study partner.
● For each exam, make a list of the topics that will come up.
● Link to learning outcomes.
● Link to course weeks.
● Link to assignment question.
● Put the lists on your wall and in your course work folders.

Predict

Once you have examined all the course information that you have been given and all the past papers that you can find – predict the questions that will come up on the exam paper attached to your programme. Then decide which questions you think you would be most interested in and that you will therefore plan to answer in the exam proper. It does help you to learn if you follow your interests and enthusiasms through a course – and, conversely, it is very difficult to learn that in which we are totally uninterested.

Tips
● Where possible, choose to do the assignment question that leads to an exam topic. (If the course booklet specifically states that if you answer an assignment question on one thing then you must answer an exam question on something else, think about working a strategy out with your study partner. For example, you can both research for two topics (say), let us call them A and B. One of you will use the A research for their assignment, the other will use the A research for the exam. And the other way round for the B research.)
● Open a revision folder on each exam **topic** that you intend to answer.

Plan

Once you have chosen your exam topics, you must plan your learning and revision strategy for each topic. This is your strategy for learning all you must know to answer an exam question on that topic – drawing on what you now know about memory and learning style. We have covered this in a list of useful things to plan to do – throughout a whole course. This is definitely not something to do just before your exams.

● **Tip:** If you want to get a really good grade you will have to do more than the basic minimum amount of work: you must read around the subject, you must think for yourself! If you only give back to tutors what you hear in class and you only use their examples and handouts – then you will only get an average grade. The choice is yours (for more information on this go to Chapter 6 – creative learning).

Things you should plan to do
1 Have a revision folder for each topic – in each exam.

2 Put relevant class, lecture and reading notes into each folder.

3 Answer assignment questions linked to exam topics.

4 Put assignment notes into the relevant folders.

5 Put the assignments into the folders.

6 Put any extra work that you do – say, following your tutor's feedback on your assignment – in the folders.

7 Put in press cuttings.

8 Start a revision cycle for each of the topics that you want to learn – from week one of each course!

9   Build a big learning and revision pattern for each topic.

10   Add information to your own 'big picture' every week.

11   Spend a few minutes reviewing your big picture every week.

12   Put key information onto index cards. Carry them with you – learn them in a supermarket checkout queue, learn them on the bus, learn them in the lift.

13   Fill in the 'Get Ready for Your Exams' checklist on page 115.

Prepare

It is not enough to plan to do well in your exams – you must actually **do** everything that you have planned to do. In this way you really will prepare for your exams. So to prepare properly you have to:

■ Keep a revision cycle going for each exam topic.

■ Keep your revision folders and your big picture revision pattern in order and up to date.

■ Go through each revision folder from time to time, throwing out excess material.

■ Each week add key points and illustrations to your big picture.

■ Keep your portable index cards up to date. As you learn the material, reduce your notes, make your index card notes shorter.

● **Tip:** Each time you make your notes shorter, you are actually revising the material.

■ Illustrate your notes with memorable cartoons.

■ Make key word tapes using rhyme and music. Play these as you go over your big picture notes.

■ Design quizzes – test your friends.

Successful exam preparation – tips and tricks

▒ **Want to do well:** be interested, know what you want from the course, know why you want to get a good grade.

▒ **Learn the bones:** only learn key word points – otherwise you fill your memory with padding. You want the skeleton, not the whole body.

▒ **Memorise:** take time each week to memorise key facts.

▶

- **Practise** turning key words into essays.

- **Study partner:** make sure you do have a study partner. Plan and prepare perfect answers together.

- **Board games!** Get a Trivial Pursuits or some other board game. Put the questions to one side. Devise question and answer cards for all your exam topics – play the game with your study partner.

- **See it, hear it, say it, do it!**

Practise

At last we have come to something that you *can* do three weeks before your exams! All the above strategies emphasise learning key data – names, dates, key points of information – from the beginning of each course. What you need to do just before the exam is to practise using the information that you are learning – under exam conditions. Typically this involves practising planning and writing essays under timed conditions.

It's different in exams

Over your programme of study you use key information in class discussion, in group based learning activities, in presentations and other assignments. You have time to plan and research your answers. You have anything from 1000 to 3000 or more words in which to answer a question. Suddenly in an exam you have just half an hour or an hour to plan and write a perfect answer.

You now have to work completely differently to the way you have worked before. As with a driving test, you will not be able to do this unless you have practised doing it. You will not be able to plan and write a good essay in a time limit unless you have practised both planning and writing under timed conditions. It is as simple as that.

Practising for exams

- Practise brainstorming and planning – develop the ten-minute brainstorm technique.

- Go through all the questions in your course handbook – allowing ten minutes per brainstorm, plan an answer for each one.

- Find past exam papers – allowing ten minutes per brainstorm, brainstorm every question on the paper.

- See how much you can write in half an hour.

- Practise writing something good in half an hour.

- Practise timed writing: when you have finished a long assignment essay – practise writing a half-hour version of the same essay.

- Practise timed writing with notes.

- Practise timed writing without notes.

- Practise preparing and writing 'perfect' answers with your study partner.

Using time in exams

Each exam is different. For each you will have to know how long the whole exam is, how many questions you will have to answer and therefore how long you will have for each question. Time per question needs to be divided between preparation time and writing time.

This will mean allocating overall exam time to:

- **Reading the paper:** Always read the questions carefully. That is another reason why it is important to see past papers so that the actual wording of the question does not intimidate or confuse you.

- **Planning each answer (allow ten minutes per plan!):** As with your assignment questions – analyse all the key words in the question – brainstorm each word in the question. Use the brainstorm to plan the answer: at the most basic level, you can number the different points in your brainstorm in the order that you think you will raise them in your essay. Always plan before you write. Time spent planning is never wasted. Time spent writing without planning can be very wasted indeed.

- **Start each answer:** You must begin to answer every question that you are supposed to.

- **Writing each answer:** You ought to divide time equally between the questions. You must write to time. Time yourself.

- **Reviewing what you have written.** A few minutes checking your answer can make a phenomenal difference to your marks!

- **This all takes practice!**

Handling the exam

Read the paper, identify which questions you will answer, then try the following:

1 Brainstorm and plan each answer before you write anything. The advantage of this is that as you brainstorm a question, you may recall additional information for another question.

2 Brainstorm/plan and write your favourite question. Then brainstorm/plan all the others and then write in order of preference. The advantage of this is that you feel good once you have a whole question out of the way.

3 Brainstorm/plan and then write one question at a time.

● **Tips**
● **Always start all the questions, never leave one out.**
● **Maximum marks are picked up at the beginning of your answers.**
● **Never answer more questions than you are asked – extra questions are just not marked.**
● **If you run out of time – refer marker to your plan and/or finish in note form. This allows you to pick up points for key facts.**
● **Always cross out material that you do not want the examiner to mark.**

And finally... examination day!

No writing on revision and exam techniques is complete without a look at the actual exams themselves. Here we are going to give some practical advice for the examination days. So whatever you normally do around exam time, next time you have an exam try to do some of the following.

Think smart – think positive

You need to mentally prepare for exams. You must want to do well – and you do have to work at believing in yourself. Read Chapter 7 on building self-confidence – but here are a few tips for examination time:

■ Remember that fear is normal – it does not mean that you cannot do well.

■ Enjoy your fear – it means you are facing a new challenge.

▶

> ■ Think positive thoughts – I can handle this! I'm looking forward to this exam! I'm so well prepared!
>
> ■ Act positive: find out what it would take to do well in your exam and then do it. Give 100%.
>
> ■ Have a positive study partner – encourage and support each other – no moaning!

Relaxation

We recommend earlier that as a student you build in stress relief activities from the beginning of your course, if not throughout your life. If you are in the habit of running or exercising, of meditating or doing yoga, then it will be easy for you to just do more of this around exam time.

If you are not in that habit, it is unlikely that you will suddenly develop good habits in the nick of time! So here we would just like to reiterate our advice – build some stress relief activities into your programme from the start. Further, if you feel that you will become sleepless around exam time, why not practise using a sleep audio-tape before the exams come up? Then your body will know how to use the tape when you really need it.

The night before

If you have been putting SQP4 techniques into practice over your course of studies, you should feel confident that you do know your material and that you can plan and write an answer in the time allowed. So the night before the exam, you should not be trying to cram in new information, neither should you be panicking.

You should be quietly confident. You may wish to go over your key word notes – whether you have them on a big pattern on the wall, index cards or summarised onto sheets of paper. You may wish to practise a few ten-minute brainstorms – but the essence is on quiet confidence and rest. Have an early night.

On examination day

Get up early and have a light breakfast – even if you do not feel like eating. Exams are hard work and you will need energy. But do not eat so much that all your blood goes to your stomach – you need a good supply getting to your brain!

Arrive at the examination room in good time. Do not cram in new information. Avoid people who are acting nervous or scared – they will only unsettle you and it is too late to help them now. Worse, we have heard of students who deliberately behave negatively in order to unsettle others so that they do badly in the exam. They feel that this increases their chances of doing well.

Make sure you have working pens and watch. Take some chocolate with you or glucose – for that extra energy boost mid exam.

Think positive thoughts. Read through the paper carefully and choose your questions with confidence. Brainstorm and plan before you write. Recall your revision notes by sight, sound or feel. Time yourself through each question – and start every question. Leave time to quickly review what you have written.

What examiners like to see

- Correct use of key words, phrases, terms and concepts from your subject.

- Questions answered in the correct format – essays where they want essays – reports where they want reports.

- Not writing 'all you know' on the topic but identifying the key words in the question and addressing those in your answer.

- Focus on the question set – appropriately drawing on course material.

- Discussing course material critically.

- Using the time well.

- Neat presentation.

After the exam

Try to avoid discussing the exam with other people – especially if you have another exam later that same day or the next day. Comparing answers with others can lead to panic – and you do not need that if you have other exams for which to prepare. If you do have another exam the following day, treat yourself to another relaxed evening and an early night.

Activity: The three minute test

Settle down and give yourself just three minutes to work through this short test.

Three minute test

Instructor: Name:
                Class:
                Period:
                Date:

Read the paper carefully before answering any questions. This is a timed test – you have three minutes to complete the paper.

1   Before answering any questions, read through the whole paper.

2   Print your name, class, time and date in the appropriate sections of this paper.

3   Draw five small squares in the bottom right hand corner of this sheet.

4   Circle the word 'name' in question 2.

5   Put an 'x' in each of the five squares.

6   Sign your name at the top of this paper.

7   In front of your name write 'YES, YES, YES'.

8   **Loudly**, so that everyone can hear you, call out your name.

9   Put a circle around question number 3.

10 Put an 'x' in the lower left-hand corner of this paper.

11 Draw a triangle around the 'x' that you have just put down.

12 In your normal speaking voice count down from ten to one.

13 **Loudly** call out, 'I am nearly finished, I have followed directions!'

14 Now that you have finished reading everything, do only questions one and two.

End of exam

Query: Well, how did you do? Were you that student bobbing up and down and calling things out? What does that tell you?

Discussion: Another name for this test is 'Can you follow directions?' It is a simple way of illustrating that you really do need to read an exam paper carefully before you start to answer the questions. The problem with not following directions in an exam could be that you do the wrong things. Typically this would be in the sort of exam that states answer one question in section A and then one in B and then choose one question from either section – or something like that. If you do not read these instructions very carefully you can answer the wrong questions and throw marks away!

(See also the study skills exam in Chapter 10.)

Activity: Get ready for exams checklist

This is a checklist that you could follow for each course that you do that has exams. Why not photocopy this checklist – then fill it in for each examination that you have to sit?

Subject..

Survey: I have:

- received course outline

- read the course aims and learning outcomes

- read through outline and thought about the course structure and design

- found and analysed past exam papers

- paper is.......hours

- I have to answer.........questions

- I know the typical language used

- I know the topics that come up every year

Question: I have thought about this programme.

I need to know.....................

I need to learn.....................

Predict: I have:

- Predicted the likely questions for this subject

- Chosen .... topics to revise in depth

Plan: I have:

- Opened a revision folder on:
    - Topic 1:............................
    - Topic 2:............................
    - Topic 3:............................
    - Topic 4:............................
    - Topic 5:............................
    - Topic 6:............................

▶

- made links between learning outcomes, course work, assignments and my revision topic

- placed course work notes, press cuttings, assignment notes and assignments into the topic folders; on a big pattern on the wall; and on my index cards

- Discovered that I prefer learning:

  - by sight

  - by sound

  - by feel/movement

- Thus my preferred revision system will utilise mainly:

  - pattern notes of the key points

  - tapes of me reciting the key points

  - making condensed charts of the key points

- I will **see it, hear it, say it, do it**

Prepare: I have:

- gone through my exam folders and have prepared condensed notes of everything that I need to remember for the exam for:

  - Topic 1:...

  - Topic 2:...

  - Topic 3:...

  - Topic 4:...

  - Topic 5:...

  - Topic 6:...

- I am learning this by:

  - memorising my key point patterns/charts

  - reciting my key points along with my tape

  - testing myself and friends

  - carrying index cards with the key points on them

- I have drawn up a revision timetable for this exam subject. It includes the following:

▶

Practising

- positive thinking

- brainstorming and planning answers

- planning and writing 'perfect' answers with friends

- writing with notes

- writing without notes

- timed writing without notes

I am ready and confident!

Conclusion

How to pass exams (big picture – small steps) links overview theory with exam success. Specifically we focused on responses to exams, how to develop your memory and utilise your learning style – and then we discussed how to draw on all these things in the SQP4 process – a whole course strategy for success. We finished with a quick look at examination day. You should now be ready to put these ideas into practice in your own learning. Do use the various checklists that have been included to help you. Good luck with your exams!

Review points

When reviewing this chapter you might realise that you now have:

- an understanding of the role of the overview with respect to assessment preparation

- a sense of how understanding exams can improve your attitude to them

- a better understanding of the role of memory in learning

- a sense of how to utilise learning style information to develop your memory and learn course material

- an introduction to SQP4 – a whole course strategy for success

- a sense of how to handle the examination day.

Further reading

If you are interested in taking the ideas in this chapter further, the following might help:

Buzan, B. and Buzan, T. (1999) *The mind map book* BBC publications, London
Buzan, T. (1989) *Use your head* BBC publications, London
Rogers, C. (1992) *Freedom to learn* Merrill, Upper Saddle River NJ
Rose, C. and Goll, L. (1992) *Accelerate your learning* Accelerated Learning Systems, Bucks.

6 How to learn creatively

Aims

To introduce you to creative aspects to learning – with a special emphasis on notemaking, brainstorming and question matrixing.

Learning outcomes

It is hoped that by the end of working through this chapter you will have:

■ realised the importance of creative learning strategies

■ been introduced to notemaking theory

■ been introduced to notemaking practice – with the emphasis on creative, pattern notes

■ been introduced to creative assignment preparation techniques – the brainstorm and the question matrix.

Introduction

Much of the advice given in this book with respect to **active learning** strategies, skills, techniques and practices is logical, rational and straightforward. Such techniques can turn learning and studying around for you so that your learning becomes effective, satisfying and successful. In this chapter we are taking this a step further. Logical strategies are fantastic, they will make all the difference in themselves – but to really shine, to go that one step further, everyone also needs to build creativity into their learning.

Why should we be creative?

Some people do not see the need to be creative in their studies. Perhaps it just seems like more hard work, perhaps they think that their subject does not need creativity – maybe they feel that this is a whole new area that they wish would just go away and leave them alone! However, we have found that students really do benefit from creative thinking. For one thing, it can make things feel lighter, for another it stretches and develops another part of you – and this is a good thing in itself. However, we would like you to feel really positive about being creative when you study, so we have gathered a few arguments here – read them through and see what you think.

Use all your brain

Buzan's work on the psychology of learning tells us that there are two parts to the brain, the logical left and the creative right. Learning strategies that are rational and logical work well with the left part of the brain, but this has its limitations. Buzan, for example, calls this monotonous learning – as in monotone, one colour learning. He criticises this learning as being ineffectual because it only utilises one half of the brain – and this means it is both limiting and boring. To exploit the way that our brains actually work, we have to involve the right side of the brain by being creative. Buzan follows his argument with advice on a notemaking technique that he calls 'mindmapping'. We will follow the argument through by exploring a creative, pattern notemaking system and brainstorming and question matrixing techniques.

Play with it

Graham Gibbs, in his work on teaching students how to learn, has another argument that connects to creative learning strategies. Gibbs tells us that the word 'knowledge', which has Greek and Norse roots, actually means to 'have sport with ideas', that is to play with ideas. If we cannot play with the ideas with which we are engaging as students, we will never be able to use them with confidence – hence we will not make them our own.

Typically when we approach new subjects we might be over-awed by them – and a natural response, as we have mentioned before, is to think something along the lines of 'Who am I to challenge all this?' And yet if we do challenge and question and generally play with ideas, we will learn them; if we do not, we will not.

This is why we encourage you to adopt a pattern notemaking system for recording your ideas, for making notes during research and in the process of brainstorming your assignments. These things are all designed to allow you to open up ideas – and to introduce elements of colour and the bizarre. They are in their very nature playful and encourage you to play with the ideas you are learning.

Active and significant learning

All the way through this text we place an emphasis on you becoming an active learner in control of your own learning. However, it can be very easy to feel trapped by the very nature of academic practice. How can you say what you want when you have to say it a certain way or you have to read so many things before you can even give an opinion of your own?

Carl Rogers, humanist, psychologist and teacher, addressed this by emphasising that significant learning takes place when students reach out for what they want and need when learning. We argue that creative approaches can help you to identify what it is that you want and need from your course. Yes, you will still have to read those set texts – and you will still have to frame your answers in certain ways... You will have to get to grips with academic practice. But getting an original angle on a question (brainstorming and question matrixing); seeking out original things to research and read; and then recording information in your own original and creative way – may help you to make the course your own.

Common sense

One last justification that we would like to offer for creative learning also touches on the notion of active learning – or the lack of it. Without a creative approach the student is in danger of becoming (or remaining) a passive learner, only using information in the way that other people have used it. Because they have not used a creative notemaking system, but have passively recorded what others have said, and the way that they have said it, these students get trapped into other people's thought processes.

If you become trapped into using information in the way that other people have used it, you are in danger of producing assignments that only give back to the tutor what s/he has said and what s/he has recommended that you read. Obviously this is neither active nor significant learning! But it gets worse.

Something that just passively parrots-back information to the tutor will at best only gain you an average grade. It is also really boring for the tutor. Imagine the tutor with 150 assignments to mark, all of them only giving back what s/he has said? Only using the examples that were used in the lecture? Only citing the books that the tutor recommended?

It is the assignment that has gone somewhere different, that has found an original example or illustration, that has put ideas together in an original way that will catch the tutor's eye, that will make them smile. And oh what a relief from reading those 149 other essays that all say the same thing! Thus at this very practical, common sense level, it is good to be creative.

How can I be creative?

Some people believe that you are either born creative or you are not – the same way that much of education is predicated upon the belief that you are either born a good student or you are not. But just as we argued that everyone can rehearse successful study techniques and thus learn how to be a good student, so we argue that everyone can learn creative learning styles and with practice become more creative. In this chapter we will go on to explore notemaking generally – and then take you through the theory and practice of a pattern notemaking system. We will also look at creative ways of approaching assignment questions – the brainstorm and the matrix.

If you have not tried these techniques before, we will be asking you to change or adapt your learning style. And, as always, you might find that change uncomfortable. No one likes to be uncomfortable, even more so perhaps in the educational context where for so many of us everything already feels so strange and uncomfortable. Try to reassure yourself that the discomfort will pass, and that the benefits of these strategies in terms of improvements in your ability to study and learn – and in the grades that you will get for your work – will more than compensate you for the discomfort that you are experiencing.

Conclusion

Here we have tried to make a case for creative learning strategies. We have looked at some of the arguments that exist with respect to creative learning – whole brain learning, playful learning, active and significant learning and in order to make a difference. We briefly introduced the creative techniques that we will cover below – pattern notes and brainstorming and question matrixing. By now we hope that you are ready to consider adopting these creative learning techniques yourself.

From notes to creative notes

In this section we are going to explore notemaking *per se*; we will then go on to make a case for a creative notemaking system, specifically pattern notes. We will then ask you to put pattern notemaking theory into practice immediately with an exercise on notemaking.

Activity: Structured brainstorm

Before you move on to the section on notemaking, spend a few minutes preparing yourself with a structured brainstorm around the following topics.

● **Tip:** When brainstorming, just look at the topic and write down any-thing that pops into your head – do not try to get things 'right', just try to capture your immediate responses.

Spend five minutes jotting down your responses to:

▦ Why do we make notes?

▦ When and where do we make notes?

▦ How do we make notes?

Once you have jotted down some thoughts of your own, compare your responses with those of some other students:

▦ Why do we make notes?

- To remember – I make shopping lists and lists of things to do

- To use the information, for example in my essays and exams

- To recall key points

▦ When and where do we make notes?

- I take notes at work, especially in meetings

- In lectures, seminars and tutorials

- When I'm reading – I'm not going to remember it all, am I?

- In the middle of the night in bed – no seriously. I often wake up and think of a really good point for my essay. So I keep a pad and pen by the bed so that I don't lose the thought

▦ How do we make notes?

- Well, I write my notes down – I know other people who tape theirs

- I take down too much information, I really hate my notes

- I take down key words, but I sometimes forget what they mean

- I make rough notes and do a shorter version later.

▶

Query: Are any of these comments similar to your own? It really does not matter if they are or not. Remember the point was to brainstorm and that is a creative activity – there is no necessary right or wrong when brainstorming. What you may get are interesting ideas that you can follow up.

Discussion: As always with the preparatory activities that we set at the beginning of our chapters, the point of this brainstorm was to get you ready for the work that is to come. This happens in two ways: first, it quickly reminds you of what you do know on the subject (remember, you are not empty!). Second, it can indicate the gaps in your knowledge – thus it can tell you what you need to get from the chapter. As we have mentioned before, you will learn more if you are reaching out for what you want and need.

● **Tip:** Always brainstorm before a class, lecture, seminar – and a piece of reading. It acts as a goalsetting, focusing device and you will get more.

Ordinary notes

Most people are aware that as students they will have to make notes of some sort. They are aware that these notes will form some sort of record of their studies and that they will need this record to help them remember key points. Maybe they intend to use the information in the notes in their assignments. So far so good.

However, we have noticed a change in student behaviour over the last few years. When we started teaching, students tended to take down too much information. They would write page after page of notes that really did try to capture everything a lecturer was saying – or everything that was in the book. But recently we have seen the student who sits through the lecture and makes no notes at all!

Now neither of these strategies is going to prove particularly successful to the student. The former because it is too passive: you do not need to take down pages and pages of information – including the lecturer's bad jokes. The latter is just ridiculous; you do need to take down some information as you study, so that you can follow it up as you undertake your own research on the subject.

What's my line?

If you do make notes you might be writing down information in a linear fashion – that is line-by-line writing – the way it is here on this page. And the 'old' student described above would feel that they had got 'really good' at notemaking if they always ended up with pages and pages of information. There would be a very reassuring feel to having captured everything.

However, there are many problems with linear notes:

- You can take so many notes you feel swamped by them.
- You take so many notes that you never use them again.
- If you cannot write really fast, you feel left out of studying.
- If you miss things, you panic and miss even more.
- If you leave things out you can feel like a failure.
- It is an exceedingly passive form of notemaking – you do not need to be able to think to make linear notes, but you do need to think to be able to learn.
- All the information looks the same, which makes it very difficult to recall specific points of information.
- It is a monotonous way of learning – Buzan's half brain learning point. It is boring and it only engages a small part of the brain, which is not a good thing.

As our whole emphasis is on active learning we are going to recommend a much more active notemaking system than the linear. Specifically we want you to consider – and then rehearse and develop – a pattern notemaking system that will improve your notemaking and your overall learning.

Creative notes – pattern notes

To build creativity and activity into your notemaking we recommend that you develop a **key word, pattern notemaking** system. As you might guess, the key word aspect implies that instead of taking down every word that is said – or every word that you read – you devise your own key words that summarise or stand for the information that you have decided that you want to keep.

It is important to reduce information to keywords; for one thing you do not need to overburden your memory by trying to remember too much data. Further, the point of gathering information, is that you learn the essence of it – then you practise **using the information for yourself** in class discussion, in presentations and in your written assignments. You want to strip back information to the basics – and learn them. They can then be the foundation to your own thinking and writing.

Beginner's guide to pattern notes

You can make key word notes from lectures and from your reading. There are several stages that you can go through – the trick is to remember that you can draft and re-draft notes. You do not need to get them right first go!

1 Get an overview of the lecture or chapter before you start. With books, you know to read the beginning and end of chapters. With lectures, you should get the sense of what the lecture is to be about from your syllabus or scheme of work.

2 Once you know what the lecture or text is about – brainstorm – identify what you know on the topic and what you need to find out.

3 Then goal set – that is, work out the sort of information that you want to take away (an overview, key points, key names and dates, key quotes…). Remember to look at your assignment question to help you here.

4 With your goals in mind, engage with the lecture or the text in an active way – searching for and identifying key words, points, etc.

5 Put the key points down in a 'rough' way first. With a book, we have suggested that you make notes on the text itself. With the lecture, you might put the title in the centre of a piece of paper and draw points away from the title. If things connect directly to the central topic, branch them off. If they connect with each other, draw them off from the sub-branches.

6 Review your rough notes – make up your mind just what you need to keep and what you do not need. Think about how to connect ideas with each other.

7 Construct your own key word pattern – adding colour, pictures and diagrams to illustrate points and to act as memory triggers.

● **Tips:**
● **The Von Rostorff effect – our minds are playful by nature and the triggers that work best with our minds are funny, dramatic, obscene or colourful (in Palmer and Pope, 1984).**
● **See Fig. 6.1 – a pattern note on pattern notes.**

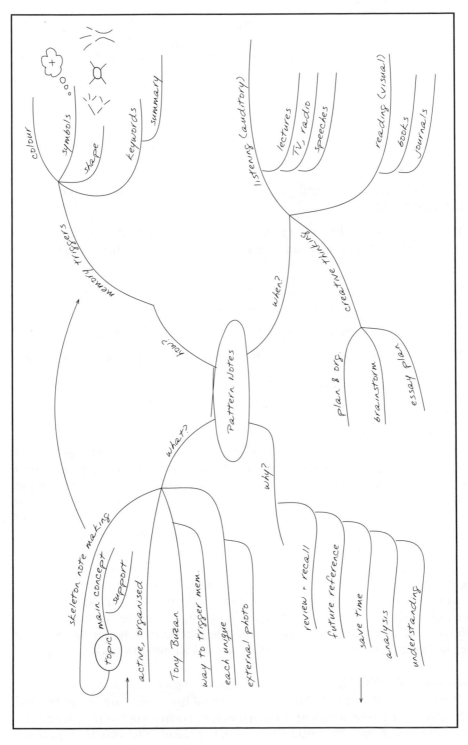

Figure 6.1 Example of pattern notes

Patterns are best

This very active, interactive form of notemaking definitely requires some practice to get used to. But when mastered, you will find that each time you make your notes you create distinctive patterns that not only record key points but also help you to learn those points.

The advantages of pattern notes are:

- Instead of taking down masses of possibly useless information, you select only that information that will be of use to you.

- They are short notes and you are inclined to re-use notes that are manageable.

- You do not need to be able to write quickly, you just need to practise selecting useful information (working in stages from rough draft to revised key word notes).

- Selecting and arranging useful information keeps you actively engaged with your information and hence you learn more.

- You can choose to make your notes interesting and memorable.

- Each set of notes looks unique – this also helps to make them memorable.

- Building colour, pictures, diagrams and unusual things into your notes engages the whole brain into your learning – thus you learn more.

But it feels so strange

As we have mentioned above, typically this involves a dramatic change in your learning style – which will need considerable practice and will involve discomfort. The trick is to take your time, and don't try to get things right first go. To get better at pattern notemaking, you will need to make mistakes and get it wrong. You will need to do rough drafts of notes that you then shorten and rearrange. And, yes, it is difficult to make short notes when you do not feel that you understand a subject – and when you do not feel confident. But, it does get easier to make those short notes when you do know and understand more.

And do remember you will not be making your notes in 'the dark'. If you follow the 'big picture' advice on gaining the overview of a course (Chapter 4) you will know what you need to do and learn to pass the course – and this should tell you what notes you need to make.

Notemaking as learning

In the first section of this book we discussed how learning could be said to be gathering new ideas and information, recording them, reorganising, understanding, remembering and using them. The creative, pattern notemaking system that we are describing here actually encourages you to reorganise the information you gather as you make sense of and record it. Thus we argue that a pattern notemaking system is beyond a mere recording system, it is a learning practice as well.

Activity: Practising pattern notes

Here we want you to practise pattern notemaking techniques. There will follow a short piece on notemaking from lectures. Prepare yourself for making pattern notes on the piece:

■ Have a piece of paper that you turn sideways, landscape fashion.

■ Have plenty of coloured pens to hand.

■ Remember your QOOQRRR techniques:

■ Question – remember why you are reading this book and what you want to get from it.

■ Overview – remember your overview of this book – think how this activity fits in with the book as a whole.

■ Overview – read the introduction and the conclusion of the piece first so that you understand what it is about.

■ Question why you are reading it and what information you would like to take away from it.

■ Read through once, marking up the text as you notice useful points.

■ Re-read – construct your key word pattern notes.

■ Review your notes and check that they are useable.

Notemaking from lectures

In this section we are going to look at active and passive learning, why we make notes and why we have lectures. We shall move on to look at how to make notes from lectures, focusing on before, during and after a lecture – and the practical mechanics of notemaking.

Active versus passive learning

With active learning the onus is on the learner to take responsibility for their own learning – and to take steps to identify and learn important information. Passive learning is a term often used to describe what happens in the unmotivated school student. When we were at school we may have felt that it was the teacher's responsibility to know what was going on and to make sure that we passed a course – we were passive participants in someone else's process. Suddenly at university everything has changed. We discover it is our responsibility to find out what we have to learn – and to take steps to learn it. We must actively take control of our own learning.

Being an active learner means choosing courses that we want to study and deciding on our own goals for all the studying that we do. It involves understanding the what, why and how of every course that we undertake and taking active steps to learn all the information on the course. In the process of learning new information, we have to familiarise ourselves with the academic practices of our subject – the language, the knowledge claims and the key people of our subject: those who have done the research and written the books that have actually shaped the subject.

If the passive learner is a passenger whose boat bobs along on top of a course, the active learner is actually swimming through the waters of the course – navigating their own path. In this context, one of the most useful tools for the active learner is an efficient notemaking system that helps them to record and learn information.

Why make notes?

We make notes to record key information. We will use the information to seed further research, that is, we will read around the topic to increase and extend our knowledge and understanding of the topic. As we do this, we will continue to make notes, recording the key data for our subject – this will involve getting to grips with the theory and practice of our subject. We will use our notes to guide our thinking and writing on the subject. Above all, our notes will actually be part of our active learning.

Why lectures?

The lecturing system in universities has been criticised for encouraging passive learning in students. The lecturer speaks and the student either records information or, more typically, ignores it. So why do we still have lectures in universities? One reason is historical – this is the way it has always been done. Another reason for the lecturing system is economics: a single lecturer can address literally hundreds of students if the technology is right.

However, there is another reason for lecturing and it is based on the fact that universities are research institutions. The idea of the lecture is to allow students to have access to some of 'the people' of their subject. Typically a lecturer is engaging in research that is designed to develop understanding and knowledge of the subject. Lectures allow the students to engage with this person – and offer a shortcut to this up-to-date information.

At the same time, no lecture is ever designed to give 'all you need to know' on the subject. Every lecture, whilst being information rich, is supposed to prompt the student to yet further research of their own. Thus the student makes notes in the lecture, recording the key data – 'facts' and people (names and dates) – with a view to reading up on these later.

Further, the lecturer is using the language of the subject. Hence the lecturer is modelling the academic practices of the subject for the student. In a lecture students can see how arguments are constructed and evidence is used. They should note this.

How to make notes

This leads us into the final part of this section – how to make notes – with a special focus on before, during, after a lecture and the practical mechanics of notemaking.

Before

The essence of good notemaking is preparation. Students should always gain an overview of a whole programme before they start attending the lectures. Once they have the big picture, they need to work out where each specific lecture fits into it. They should also know – or work out – how the lecture will be preparing them to meet specific learning outcomes and assessment criteria. They should determine which part of the assignment a particular lecture will help them with.

Immediately before a lecture, the student should recall their overview of the course and then brainstorm for a couple of minutes to get focused on, and tuned in to, the specific lecture itself.

Typically this would involve considering for just a couple of minutes:

■ What do I already know on this subject?

■ How does this lecture relate to the assignment?

■ What do I need from this lecture?

During

After active preparation, the student must stay actively tuned into the lecture. They need to listen for the key data and select key points – names, dates, information. These should be quickly jotted down – perhaps drawing connections between points. If something previously heard or read on the subject is remembered, the student should jot down that as well. Code systems can help – as can exclamation or question marks and scrawling down the names of the important people.

Experiences in lectures may be very similar to new academic reading experiences. At first everything will be new and unknown; there will be a tendency to write down too much information. Eventually the student will build up a foundation of knowledge – and thus it will be easier to make short notes that still add to the sum of information already recorded.

After

After every lecture the active student should do something with their notes. The first thing that can be done is to make time to do short, dynamic and memorable versions of the notes. Buzan argues that unless we do something with our notes, we will forget 98% of the information in just three weeks. So, it is important to start a revision cycle as soon after completing a set of notes as possible.

As we should always treat our lecture notes as first draft rough notes, the time that is invested in refining and illustrating key word patterns does in fact become the first stage of that revision cycle.

Another simple active form of revision is to discuss the lecture with a study partner. Discussion really is the simplest way of improving understanding of a topic.

Further, students would profit from getting into the habit of actively comparing notes with one another. This is a very useful strategy not only in terms of checking and revising notes, but more than that; knowing that this will happen can actually help the student to relax a bit more during the lecture itself. After all, it is not terrible to miss something – someone else will have captured it.

After the lecture – and the review and revision of notes – every student should then goal set. That is, they should decide what to read or what to do in the light of what they have just heard. It is always a good idea to book these activities on a calendar or in a diary. If it is not booked it tends not to get done.

Finally the student should take a moment to reflect on exactly what they have learned from the lecture. Making learning conscious helps the learning process.

The practical mechanics of notemaking

As said, rough notes are made during the lecture. These are the student's own notes and they should be in any form that helps the student feel comfortable. However, there should always be an attempt to summarise or to use key words – otherwise information will be missed or the student will just be too passive.

Typically with pattern notes, the topic is written in the centre of the paper, then the pattern is constructed as lines are drawn out from the centre. One word per line – with the more important words forming the branches, which keep sub-dividing into twigs and twiglets of information.

Wherever possible, it is advisable to use a memorable illustration instead of a word, or to make a word more memorable in some way. Use of colour and highlighting can make points leap off the page.

Notes have to reach out and catch the student's eye. They have to say: 'This is important...' 'This is relevant...' 'This is related...'. Notes should clearly indicate key facts and less important ones. This struggle to identify and connect topics is the organising and understanding process.

Highly recommended is the use of pattern notes to construct whole course or whole module patterns. Thus after every lecture, students could spend some time adding points from the lecture to the big picture that they are building on the wall at home.

Conclusion

So we have looked at active learning and linked that to active notemaking. We moved on to consider the role of the lecture in student learning. We considered the fact that lecturers are often researchers – thus they give students a shortcut to cutting edge information. At the same time, lectures do not give 'all you need to know' on a subject – but they do seed personal research.

We considered how to actively engage with lectures before, during and after each lecture. Finally we quickly explored how to make pattern notes – and we suggested the build up of a whole course pattern which can be added to week by week.

Query: Have you made your pattern notes yet? If not, please attempt to do so before moving on. Do not be afraid of making mistakes. There are no mistakes, only rough drafts! The only way to avoid making mistakes is to do nothing at all – and that really is not an option if you want to be a successful student.

Once you have made your own notes, compare them with the pattern supplied (see Fig 6.2). What do you think? Are you happy with your notes? I bet that they are not bad for a first attempt. What are you going to do now to improve? Mark some time in your diary for developing your notemaking.

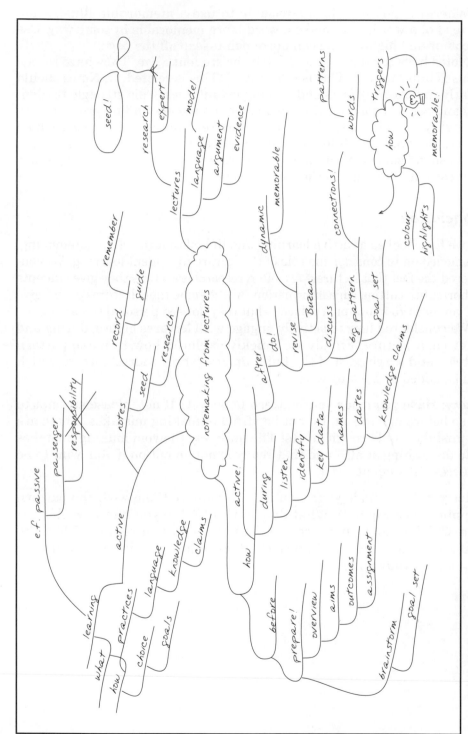

Figure 6.2 Example of a pattern of notemaking from lectures

● **Tips:**

● Why not make pattern notes for each topic in this book? This will definitely give you the practice that you need to get started.

● Make pattern notes of television and radio programmes. More practice – without the stress of it being vital for success in your own subject.

● Visit other people's lectures and make pattern notes in those. Again there is no stress – just practice.

Conclusion

So we have examined notemaking looking at both ordinary notes and pattern notes. We particularly wanted to make a good case for pattern notes so that you felt persuaded to develop them for yourself. In order to start this process off, we included an exercise on notemaking. So now it is up to you – will you continue to use this system?

Creative approaches to assignments

We have already advised brainstorming as a preparatory focusing exercise, designed to help you notice what you do and do not know on a topic about which you are to read or have a lecture. Indeed, we have practised these brainstorms with you several times already – from your original goal setting questionnaire to all the little brainstorms inserted just before a new topic in this book. Now we are going to explore how you can use this creative technique when approaching your assignments – specifically we will look again at brainstorming and move on to consider question matrixing.

The brainstorm

The idea behind the brainstorm is to open up the creative side of your mind. Typically it involves the use of a word association process that operates without censorship and preconceptions. We have already used the brainstorming device as a focusing activity – remember the 'What do I already know on this topic? What do I need to know?' questions? Therefore you should have started to familiarise your brain with this technique. When using brainstorming on an assignment topic, the strategy is to brainstorm all the key words in the question – allowing as many ideas as possible to float into your mind.

The trick is to respond immediately and not to censor your thoughts. Sometimes a thought might appear silly, irrelevant or frivolous. It may be that the thought seems odd, with no place in an academic context. Yet – it may be just that silly or odd thought that leads you on to a really bright or original idea.

Following up that idea is what will make your assignment clever, even unique. When our work has that spark of originality, when it is that bit different from all the other assignments that are dropping on to a tutor's desk, then we may gain the attention of the tutor – we may even gain a higher mark.

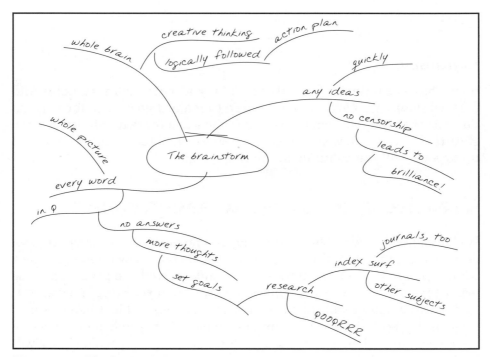

Figure 6.3 The brainstorm

Beginner's guide to brainstorming the question

Try this brainstorming strategy with all your assignments. The trick with an assignment question is to brainstorm every single word in the question.

1 Write the whole question in the middle of a really large sheet of paper – A1 is best.

2 Do not abbreviate the question. Any word that you do not write is a research avenue that you do not explore – this could well mean marks that you have thrown away.

3 Look at all the words in the question. Circle or underline the key words. Draw a line from each word.

4 Write anything and everything that comes to mind when you look at a word.

5 When you have finished, move on and do the same to another word. Keep this up until you have tackled all the words in the question.

6 Then go round again – even more ideas might pop out.

● **Tips:**
● **Do this with a study partner.**
● **It gets easier with practice.**
● **Practise ten-minute brainstorms with every question in your module/course handbook. Choose to actually answer the question that gave you the most interesting brainstorm.**

Activity: Practice brainstorm

We have given you a very small study skills question to practise on:

▓ Write the question out for yourself – in the middle of a large sheet of paper.

▓ Underline the key words.

▓ Then brainstorm (jot down all those ideas) for about ten minutes.

▓ When you have finished, compare your brainstorm with ours.

▓ Remember two things:

   1 There is no right or wrong when it comes to the brainstorm.

   2 Brainstorming, like most other skills, gets easier with practice.

The question: **Evaluate the usefulness of pattern notes to a student.**

Query:

▓ How do you feel it went for a first attempt?

▓ What will you do next?

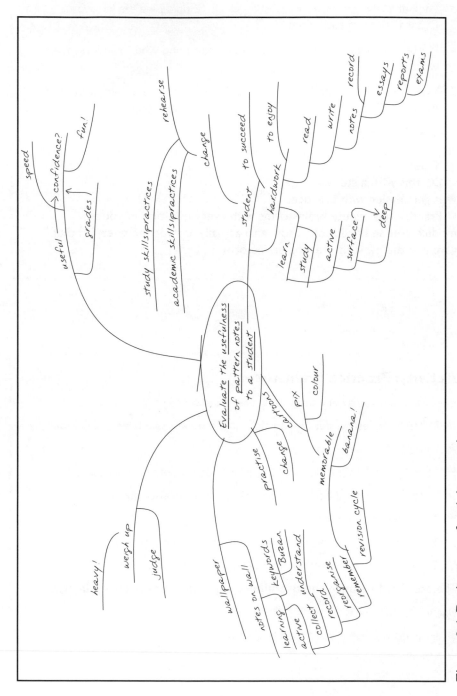

Figure 6.4 Brainstorm of activity question

The question matrix

Like the brainstorm, the question matrix (QM) is designed to open up a question – and hopefully let some creativity in. Some people see the QM as a more structured form of brainstorm.

As with the brainstorm, when using a QM you should write the whole question out, underline all the key words, then generate a question matrix off each word. Typically this involves turning all the key words into a series of smaller questions. You can then research or investigate around all the smaller questions. This research will lead you to gather the information that **will** lead to the answering of the assignment question.

When generating our smaller questions it is quite useful to use the journalism questions (five Ws and an H):

- Who
- When
- What
- Why
- Where
- How

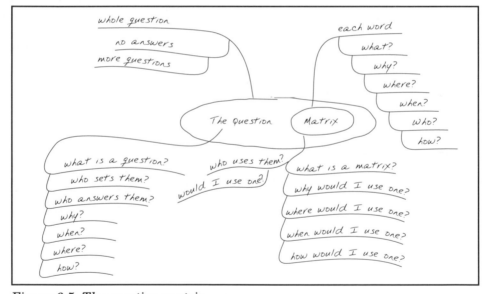

Figure 6.5 The question matrix

Activity: Draw up a question matrix

You have already performed a brainstorm – now use the who, what, when, where, why and how questions to unpack the following question. Then compare your results with the example below. Note, the QM technique gets easier with practice.

We have given a very small study skills question to practice on:

- ▨ Write the whole question out in the middle of a very large sheet of paper.
- ▨ Underline the key words.
- ▨ QM all the key words.
- ▨ When you have finished compare your QM to our (Figure 6.6).
- ▨ Remember – it will get easier with practice

The question – **Evaluate the usefulness of positive thinking to a student**.

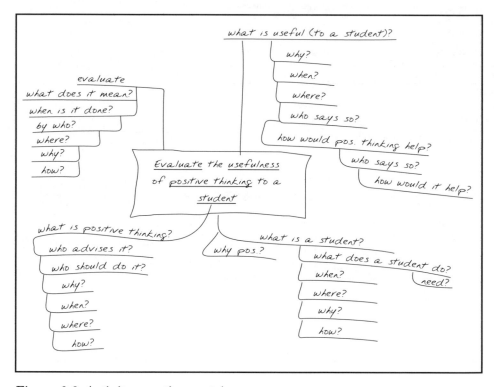

Figure 6.6 Activity question matrix

Query

- ▨ How do you feel after a first attempt?
- ▨ What will you do next?

How did it go?

Once you have completed your first attempts at brainstorming and question matrixing here, move on to use these creative techniques on your assignment questions. Once you have tried the process for a while, remember to reflect on how the strategies worked for you.

Reflection questions:

■ What has brainstorming/question matrixing been like?

■ What do you like about these techniques?

■ What do you dislike about these techniques?

■ What will you do next?

■ When will you do it?

Activity: Keep practising!

We have argued that both brainstorming and question matrixing techniques do get easier with practice. The best thing that you can now do is to use these techniques a lot.

● **Tip:** These activities work much better with a study partner or a study group.

1 Go to one of your module/course handbooks – preferably one that offers a range of questions from which you have to choose an assignment to do.

2 Choose between three and six questions to work on.

3 Allow yourself ten minutes per question for either a brainstorm or a question matrix. Remember the journalism questions: who, when, what, why, where and how.

4 When you have finished, reflect again – how do you now feel about these techniques?

Conclusion

We have argued that brainstorming and question matrixing can help you to open up your assignment questions so that you approach them creatively – and hence bring something extra to your work. You have also practised both techniques. It is now up to you to put them into practice with all your course work.

Chapter conclusion

This chapter has dealt with the notion of bringing creativity into your learning process. We looked at the importance of playing with ideas when learning – and stressed that creative techniques will help you be active in your own learning. We further argued that creativity can promote significant learning and also, because it helps you to feed your own originality into your assignments, it facilitates a sense of ownership. We introduced you to a pattern notemaking system – and you should have practised that at least once by now! Finally we looked at how brainstorming and question matrixing techniques, as creative processes, can really open up an assignment so that you will cover the whole question – in a creative way.

This section of the book is deceptively short! Do not be fooled by that! So many students have told us that pattern notes have changed their lives – and their grades – and that brainstorming meant that they actually **saw** the question for the first time. It is now up to you to try these things for yourself and see.

Review points

When reflecting on this chapter you might notice that:

- you do realise the potential of creative learning strategies

- you have practised pattern notes – and it wasn't so bad

- you have practised creative assignment preparation techniques – the brainstorm and the question matrix – and you will now use them on all your assignments in the future.

Further reading

If you are interested in taking the ideas in this chapter further, you might try the following:

Buzan, B. and Buzan, T. (1999) *The mind map book* BBC publications, London

Buzan, T. (1989) *Use your head* BBC publications, London

Gibbs, G. and Makeshaw, T. (1992) *53 Interesting things to do in your lectures* Technical and Educational Services, Bristol.

Palmer and Pope (1984) *Brain Train: studying for success* Arrowsmith, Bristol

Rogers, C. (1992) *Freedom to learn* Merrill, Upper Saddle River NJ

Rose, C. and Goll, L. (1992) *Accelerate your learning* Accelerated Learning Systems, Bucks.

7 How to build your confidence

Aims

To consider the human element of the academic environment – with a particular focus on building self-confidence.

Learning outcomes

It is intended that after reading this chapter and engaging in the activities set you will have:

- reviewed the nature of the academic environment

- discussed from where fear and a lack of self-confidence might stem

- considered the importance of self-confidence and assertiveness for you as a student

- explored some steps that you might take to improve your own self-confidence and assertiveness in the academic environment.

Introduction

In earlier chapters we have touched upon the human element of being a student in terms of motivation and commitment, stressing that in order to do well you must want to succeed and you must be able to see yourself as succeeding. We emphasised that your success would depend on you negotiating the academic practices of your subject – finding out and then building on the knowledge that already exists; discovering the key 'people'; and mastering the argument and evidence modes in your subject. How does all this make you feel? Well, in this chapter we are exploring further elements of the human dimension of being a student – in particular we will be looking at the roles that fear and positive thinking can play in student success.

Fear and positive thinking

First day experiences

'Panicky! Suddenly it hits you, because you feel that everyone is looking at you, which is stupid because no one is looking at you. But I remember coming up the steps and all these people sitting down and I felt everybody was staring at me and saying, why is that old woman coming here?'

'I felt very self-conscious – and terrified that I couldn't find the room. I saw this enormous building and it really scared me … It's frightening.'

'So I get half way through and I say, why, why, why can't I just be happy going to work and going home? Why did I start this? I can't bear it! …'

'I was desperate – I was very nervous. And, the more nervous you are, the less you pick up things. You can't listen and you want everything to go in and nothing's going in. So the first [module] was awful. …'

'I was quite frightened and I think most of the students were as well! And after I spoke to and got to know a few students we realised that – even though some of the students were sounding confident – they were quite anxious and worried and frightened themselves.'

'It was really nerve racking sitting in this room… I did feel nervous, but I thought you're here now, they can't kill you and you can run away if you don't like it.'

So now you're a student

As someone who has chosen to be a student, you have entered an academic environment that may or may not seem strange to you. You have committed yourself to a programme of study – as such, you will be expected to understand the nature of your subject and what is involved for you as a student of that subject. You will be expected to attend lectures and seminars; you will be expected to undertake independent research, to read around your subject. As part of making material your own, you will be expected to make useable notes of what you see, hear and do. From time to time you will be expected to demonstrate your learning in assignments – written and oral – and in exams. Whilst the overall goal of all this activity is that you become a confident initiate into your subject, many of the stages and processes involved in becoming this new, confident person can actually feel quite intimidating. Many people are so intimidated that they give up on study altogether. In this section we are going to explore this all too human dimension of studying.

Yes, actively developing study and academic skills and practices has a significant impact on student self-confidence – and this is the goal of much of this book. But our work with students has shown us that actively focusing on and building self-confidence and self-esteem in students can directly and dramatically affect student achievement – and that is our goal now. It is the intention of this section to reduce anxiety by introducing you to strategies for increasing self-confidence and self-esteem in the academic environment. Thus we will explore the possibility that self-confidence can have a direct impact on student success. We will move on to examine what causes fear and why we experience fear. Finally we will explore some very practical things to do to overcome fear and build self-confidence and self-esteem.

Confidence and study skills make a difference

The Guardian (13 January 1998) reported a research project at Oxford University that investigated why, given the universal high A' level qualifications of the student intake, some students went on to get first class degrees whilst others did not.

They found that different students had very different *attitudes* to studying. More importantly, typically it was the students lacking in self-confidence who achieved the lower grades.

Students speak up

Here are some comments by the students quoted above after a few weeks and having had an opportunity to learn and rehearse their study and academic skills:

'It is part of my life now. In fact I think I'm quite sad, because when the essay's done and handed in I have to go and put the computer on and stroke it.'

'I had some anxieties … that were partly about my writing skills and structuring essays and a few other things… I had a lot of anxiety over that… So I came to study skills. And it all started making sense and when it made sense it all fell into place. And it sort of opened up a new world of knowledge for me as well…'

'Because in the beginning you are all so shy and you're all very conscious, but as I said, we all feel the same, but because we don't talk to each other we don't know that the other person feels exactly the same… Now, it's a great feeling, you belong now; you are part of the university. The whole thing belongs to me. It's my university now.'

Does it affect our work?

Do you think that a runner will achieve more by running along thinking 'I am a failure, I cannot possibly win!' or 'I am a success, I see myself winning this race!'? I think that most of us would agree that the runner who thinks and feels like a success has more chance of winning a race than the one who thinks and feels like a failure. Of course the physical conditions have to be there – the training, the diet etc., but basically for the runner to do well s/he must want to do well and must believe that it is possible to do well: s/he must have self-belief and self-confidence.

What is true for the runner is also true for students. You must want to do well and believe that it is possible for you to do well. You must have self-belief and self-confidence. Yes, the study and academic skills and practices have to be learned and rehearsed, but a positive mental attitude will mean that you can become successful.

What, even at university?

Human beings are rounded – they are made up of many facets: cognition/intellect/effect **and** emotion/feelings/affect. Our intellect and our emotions can both play a part in every aspect of our lives, including that of being a student. There is a danger in thinking that because studying is an academic, intellectual activity, there is no room for the emotional dimension. But you cannot abolish part of yourself as a human being just because it does not seem to fit. In fact it can be the very ignoring of our emotional side that causes the problem; for what we ignore or deny, we cannot deal with.

There are many things in the educational environment that will affect you emotionally as a student – and as a human being. We hope that some of them will excite, stimulate and even thrill you. Others may frighten, intimidate or horrify you. It is important to notice what is happening to **your** feelings when you are studying. Where possible, try to do something about your feelings as a student. Ideally it is advisable to harness your positive feelings and work to overcome your negative ones.

Activity: Thinking about studying

Take a few moments to think about the following statement – then write down your **reactions** to the statement.

> 'It is in order to return at this point to Jameson's "loss of the referent" theme, because it is precisely this phenomenology of the everyday that Jameson's work both lacks and consciously relegates to the ethnographic sidelines.' (Feather, H, 2000, Intersubjectivity and contemporary social theory p135)

Now compare your reactions with those gathered from some other students:

▶

▓ I got really really angry! Why on earth do they have to write like that? It's stupid.

▓ This is strange and scary; but it's where I've got to get to.

▓ I read it several times trying to make sense of it.

▓ I used my dictionary of literary terms and tried to make sense of it piece by piece.

▓ It made me feel like giving up, it's obvious that I'm not welcome here.

▓ Well I just laughed and laughed. They've got to be joking, haven't they?

Query:

▓ Were any of these reactions like your own?

▓ What do you notice about these reactions?

▓ Perhaps you noticed that there was a whole range of reactions to the statement?

Discussion: Now we are not arguing that there are right or wrong reactions – just different ones. However, when we are in particular situations, we often feel that our feelings about those situations – and our reactions to them – are the only possible feelings and the only possible reactions. We do not know that there is any choice involved at all. Surely, if such and such happens, the only possible response is...?

And yet you can see from the students we spoke to that what moves one student to fury makes another laugh. What makes one student resolved to progress makes another feel as though they ought to give up.

Once we realise that reactions to situations can vary, then we can begin to realise that there might be some choice involved in how **we** react. Once we get there we can start to work on our own reactions to situations – especially our negative reactions.

Activity: Thinking about positive thinking – SWOT analysis

Take a few moments to think about your positive thinking and your reaction to the proposition that you might be able to affect your own responses to education:

▓ Strengths: what are you confident about?

▓ Weaknesses: what are you unconfident about?

▓ Opportunities: what do you feel about developing your self-confidence? What opportunities are there in this for you as a student?

▓ Threats: do you feel threatened by the thought of changing your reactions? What are the dangers in this to you as a student?

▶

When you have completed this activity, discuss your responses with your study partner.

Discussion: Perhaps you noticed that there are opportunities for you in developing your positive thinking? You might have realised that a positive attitude will help you face academic tasks as challenges rich with opportunity.

On the other hand, you might be a bit frightened of changing. Change is uncomfortable. Maybe you are used to doing okay in your work but the thought of success terrifies you, for you do not know all the implications of this for you. That is okay! Change will mean entering the unknown – and success may well be a new experience for you – but you can learn to face this positively as well!

(Note: If you have identified areas that look as though they might give you real problems or cause for concern – go to see someone at your college or university: for example, your personal or academic tutor, the study support people or the counselling service.)

The feeling student

The activities above are designed to illustrate that as human beings our feelings will play a role in our lives as students. We have also argued that negative feelings might actually prevent us from working to our best ability. Further we have considered that changing our reactions may not be entirely problem free – but that does not mean that you should not do it! Let us now move on to explore the role of fear in our lives, in particular we will look at what we are frightened of, where fear comes from – and things to do to build self-confidence.

What are you frightened of?

So what are we actually frightened of? I'm not talking about phobias here (like a crippling fear of spiders or heights), but the sorts of things that make you feel uncomfortable or that you tend to avoid; things that make you sweat or cause you the odd sleepless night and so forth.

All human beings are frightened of many things. Typically we are all frightened of the new; we are frightened of change. We may be frightened of ageing, disease and death. More mundanely we may be frightened of picking up the telephone...of entering a library...of writing our first essay...of giving a presentation...of anything and everything. All these fears are completely normal and yet they can be very inconvenient for us as human beings – and especially awkward for us as students.

Let's face it, to undertake to become a student is to undertake to change. But this change does involve risk – we do not know all the implications of these changes for us as human beings. Risk **is** frightening. Yet the only way to avoid risk is to do nothing at all – and this really is not an option for you either as a student or as a human being.

It's just me!

It could be argued that there is another dimension to this fear, and that is that whenever we are frightened at school, college or university we tend to feel that we are the only ones that are frightened. We feel alone in our fear – and that just makes it feel worse. We look at other people and they look fine – they don't feel what we feel. This is especially true for new students. When we ask new students how they are feeling, they all say that they are scared. And every scared one thinks that they are the only one carrying this shameful burden.

Tutors as students

'I had been teaching for many years when I took a higher degree programme. All the students on the programme were lecturers like myself – and I thought that they all knew what they were doing – but I did not.

'When I sat down in my first seminar and the tutor asked us a question, I went red, my heart pounded so much I felt that everyone else must hear it – and I absolutely would not volunteer a comment – I was too frightened to look, sound or feel a fool. I found myself experiencing exactly the same fears as my students. The fact that I was also a tutor did not help at all.

'Later in the course another student asked, "What on earth does 'overarching syntagmatics' mean?" We all looked at each other – we all laughed. We realised that none of us knew – and that we had all been too scared to admit it. We then decided to do something about this.

'It was most probably easier for us as tutors to do something about our fears. For once we knew we all had the same fears – we did know what to do. We had an idea of what might work for us as students.

What we did

- formed study groups
- met to discuss our thoughts on the difficult texts we had to read
- read one anothers' draft essays to give critical feedback
- read one anothers' finished essays to get extra ideas for our exams.

Suddenly the whole course was more enjoyable – and all our experiences were more positive.'

Discussion: What worked for the lecturer above can work for you. This is why we continually urge you to work with a study partner – and why we are going to explore group/team work in Chapter 8.

We are in all the same boat

From our experiences as students, as tutors and as tutors who are also students, we can assure you that everyone tends to feel fear when they start studying. It is normal to be scared of the challenge of becoming a student. It is natural to feel scared if you do not feel like an academic. It is not shameful – it does not mean that you are not cut out for studying – and you really, really are not alone. Everyone else is feeling just the same as you.

Activity: The fearful student

■ Can you think of any situation where you have let your fears stop you?

■ What do you think about that now?

■ Are there any aspects of your studying that fill you with fear?

■ Why don't you – and your study partner – make a list of all the things that frighten you about studying; then score each item on your lists from 0–9 depending on how fearful they make you? Compare lists with each other.

■ What do your lists tell you about yourselves?

■ What do they tell you about your fears?

One of the most liberating things about this exercise is to realise that you are not alone in your fear. It can also be reassuring that people have different fears from you. Make some notes to yourself about what you gained from this exercise.

Self-help books

As with everything else here in this book, you may like to follow up some of the ideas that you find here on positive thinking by reading some more on your own. There are many positive thinking books in bookshops and libraries that are all dedicated to helping people overcome their fears and in the process to learn how to face life's challenges more positively. Some of these may appeal to you and we know that one of the ones that our students particularly like is Susan Jeffers (1987) *Feel the fear and do it anyway*.

● **Tip:** When doing extra reading you will find that you like some books more than others, that you like some authors' writing style – but you definitely do not like the way others write at all. That is okay, the trick is to experiment until you find something that does appeal to you.

However, we have written this section of the book to introduce you to the ideas of positive thinking such that you can begin to change things for yourself right away. In particular we are looking at the relationship between fear and self-confidence.

Believe in yourself

The overarching theme of most positive thinking books is that fear boils down to a lack of self-confidence and a lack of faith in ourselves. The argument is that we fear things because we believe that we will not be able to cope with them. We think life will defeat us. And yet consider the things that we do achieve as human beings.

We managed to learn our language. We learned how to walk. We learned the behaviour that was expected of us in different situations – in the family, with our friends, in school, at work. We managed to go to school and survive that. Many of us then went on to get jobs – maybe even raise families. All of these activities and many more we did eventually take in our stride – no matter how much we feared them beforehand.

Overall we tend to be much more resilient than we give ourselves credit for. In the end, whatever life chooses to throw at us – we cope with it. Sometimes we even cope spectacularly well. All we tend to do by doubting ourselves is actually make it more difficult to cope – not easier. Surely it is not life that we need to fear, but fear itself? All we do when we listen to – or, worse, give in to – our fears is to damage our own lives.

Think about it

Can you remember times when you have worried and worried over a particular thing, perhaps for months – even for years – then the thing happened?

- What was it like?

- What about all the things that you worried about that did not happen?

- What was that like?

Discussion: It is said that 90% of what we worry about just does not happen at all. It is really silly to spend our lives worrying. So one thing to gain from looking at positive thinking is an outlook that can improve your whole life, not just your life as a student. But at the moment we are looking at this with respect to being a student. Being a student can be scary, especially as many of the things that we worry about will actually happen to us. We will have to understand the subject and make those notes. We will have to write those essays and give those presentations. Becoming more positive about yourself will help you as a student!

Students do it in the dark

So what effect does this worry have – does it make us better students? Well in our experience the typical answer is no.

We worry about exams so much that we are too scared to prepare for them. Surprise, surprise – we always do badly in our exams.

We worry about the final assessment on a course so much, we are too frightened to look at the question. Suddenly instead of having 15 weeks to slowly work on the assignment and really get to grips with it – we only have two days to prepare the assignment. And, no, we do not achieve the best mark possible for that assignment.

We worry about that presentation that we have to give for six months – it spoils our days and nights – our whole lives. Suddenly it is over! We did not go up in a puff of smoke – we found that we survived after all!

What was the point of all that worry? All it does is blight your life. And it literally blights your life as a student, for it means that you do not give of your best and you do not work to your best advantage.

We have to learn to pass though our fear – not to live with it.

Why do we experience fear?

But, you might argue, surely this fear is there for a purpose? If not, where does it come from? Why do we have it? Both evolutionary psychology and popular (pop) psychology (in the form of the self-help book) have something to say in this debate.

Simon Baron Cohen (1997) argues that fear, anxiety and even depression are a legacy of our animal evolution. He points out that when an animal is on unfamiliar territory it is in danger of its life. As human beings we have a memory of this fear so that we are also frightened when on unfamiliar territory. But more than that, as humans we have a consciousness. Consciousness means that we are aware of our reactions and responses in ways that no animal is. Birds looking around nervously on a bird table are not aware that they are nervous. They just are.

However as conscious human beings, we are aware of our own nervousness and fear. We can focus on and really be obsessive about our fears – this is what makes fear so dangerous for us.

Remember, to be human is to constantly move into unfamiliar territory. This means that we are constantly moving into fearful situations. The more we focus on our *fear response* rather than the situation, the more we are in danger of avoiding the things that make us frightened. We need to be able to face our fears in order to deal with the unfamiliar – and grow.

The self-help book tends to have a slightly different attitude to fear: Jeffers (*op cit.*), for example, argues that we are accidentally **taught** fear in the way that we are brought up. You might remember:

- Mind how you cross the road.

- Don't go climbing that tree.

- Don't talk to strangers.

- Don't go too fast.

- Are you sure you can manage that?

- Let me do that for you.

Sound familiar? Do you have any of your own from your own upbringing?

When people say these things to us they are really just expressing their fear (I don't want anything bad to happen to you); but what we hear, and internalise, is that they think that we are inadequate. This can have far reaching consequences. It can be terribly damaging to our self-confidence to feel that the person who loves us most in the world, the person who really knows us, does not think much of us. They must think we are pretty useless if they believe that we cannot even cross the road without their advice!

The fear within

Over the years, Jeffers argues, the external warning voice of our carers becomes our own internal negative voice. We no longer need anyone else to criticise and doubt us – we can do it for ourselves. Eventually it can be that every time we are faced with something new a little voice pipes up inside saying: Watch out! Why are you doing that? You'll only fail! You'll only look silly...

This can be especially so if you are a student, for there will be so many new things to face – and if we see them all only as opportunities to fail, we will never get the most from them. Further – consider the role of mistakes in our learning. We really do have to learn by a process of trial and error – by making mistakes and learning from them. But if the thought of making mistakes makes us feel so bad that we feel like giving up, we are not going to do well! We have to work to overcome this. Face studying as an adventure, and realise that you will live through your mistakes and learn from them.

But I'm not really an academic

An accent on fear and a lack of self-confidence can be particularly harmful if you are a student but you do not feel like a student. If you are in an academic environment and you do not feel like an academic. And given that these days more and more 'non-traditional' students are entering into higher education, this could be an issue affecting a very high proportion of students indeed. If this does describe how you are feeling right now, **you** will have to work to overcome your own negative feelings. You **are** a student. You have been accepted onto a degree programme. If you are interested and motivated – and you do the work – you can succeed, and you will grow into the role of academic.

Do these thoughts on fear make any sense to you? Can you now review the fears that you noted before in a different light? Make some notes to remind yourself and read on.

Can we do anything to overcome fear and build self-confidence?

Obviously the whole tone of this section – as with the book as a whole – is leading you to believe that you can do something about this state of affairs. Here we are going to take a leaf out of the self-help type book and look at re-framing fear; taking responsibility for our lives; adopting a positive vocabulary; making positive friends; and utilising positive statements.

Re-framing fear

We have argued above that fear, whilst often uncomfortable, is a perfectly natural and normal response to life – especially to new or unfamiliar situations. What we can do is change our responses to that fear. Fear does not have to mean run and hide under the duvet; it can actually mean something completely different. Here are some new ways to look at fear: see if they help you at all.

■ **Fear is good:** Fear is okay, it is part of growth and doing new things. Fear does not mean, 'This is not for me!'. Instead fear means that you are doing something new, you are facing a new challenge, you are taking a risk – and that is okay too, because that is all part of growing and changing. Thus when we feel fear we should celebrate the fact that we are growing and changing. This is a good thing, not a bad one.

■ **Fear affects everyone:** Fear really does affect everyone and realising that we are not alone in our fears can actually help. If Cohen is to be believed, everyone feels fear when on unfamiliar territory. Everyone experiences fear when they do something new. Realising that we are not alone in our fears can take away the stigma of fear, it does not mean that we are cowards, just that we are human. Once we accept this we can move on.

■ **The only way to get rid of the fear of something is to do it ... the quicker the better:** The only way to move on might be to do what we fear, for the only way to get rid of the fear of doing something is to do it – quickly. You know that this is true. You can spend months worrying about something, and then it takes two minutes to do it! Let's get rid of those months of worry – do it now: you know it makes sense!

■ **It is easier to face fear than to live with it:** It really is easier to do what we fear than to keep living with the fear. Again, I bet that you know this is true already. The more we give in to fear the more fearful we become. So every time you decide to face a fear, remind yourself that this is not a hardship – you are taking the easier option.

■ **It takes practice:** Re-framing fear in these ways may not come naturally to you. However, with practice you will find that you can face fear differently, and it will make a big difference – especially to the way that you face the challenge of being a successful student.

We can take responsibility for our own lives

As well as re-framing fear, we can re-frame our whole lives. One way of doing this is to really embrace responsibility for ourselves. What do you think this means? We argued above that we can begin to take responsibility for our emotional response to events. Just because something normally makes us angry, or scared or whatever, does not mean that it has to continue to do so. We can work on our responses to events and try to change our instinctive (or learned) responses and do something else. One of the most powerful things that we can do is to take responsibility for our own lives.

I'm not a number

Taking responsibility means dropping forever a victim mentality: the 'It's not my fault, it's his or hers or theirs!' syndrome. Now we all know that neither society nor nature is necessarily fair. But if we keep blaming everyone else for what happens to us, we end up being trapped in circumstances, instead of being able to rise above them. And if we become trapped by life's events, we are the ones that suffer – no one else!

Remember, if it's **their** fault, there is nothing **I** can do to change things. If it's my responsibility, then there is something that I might be able to do to take control of events. I can look to see what I can do – what I can change – what effect I can have. This is really important as a student. Look at your course, look at the work that you have to do – and do something about it. Learn how to learn and study more effectively – if you have not already done so, make use of the advice in the rest of this book. All that advice is designed to make you more effective and more successful as a student.

So start right now, try saying, **I am responsible**:

■ for my decisions

■ for my actions

■ for getting my work in on time

■ for getting good grades...

If these things matter to us we can take steps to make them happen. It may take hard work and sweat, but we can do it. If we don't do it, perhaps it is because these things do not really matter to us, we just say they do because it is expected of us, because it is what our parents, friends or partners want for us or because it makes us look good? In the end, we will only do well in our studies if it is what we want. It is our work that has to make it happen, not anyone else's.

So the next time you find yourself blaming someone, anyone, for something that **you** are not doing, stop and think again. What can **you** do to make it happen?

Develop a positive vocabulary

A really good way to develop a positive and responsible outlook is to develop a positive vocabulary. Just as we can re-frame fear so that it does not mean what it used to mean, we can also change the way that we talk about the world. Here we are going to look at problems, disasters – and choice.

'It's an opportunity'

A simple, unconscious negative framing of the world is when we always see new tasks or events as problems rather than opportunities. When we do this we tend to always focus on the negative in any event rather than on the possible good that will come out of it. Most people do this much of the time – but it is a very unhelpful way of viewing the world, making everything we do do seem that much harder. Imagine starting a new job – would you see that as a wonderful opportunity to meet new people and face new challenges? Or do you see it as more hard work? Do you just see how difficult it will all be?

The instant negative response can be especially damaging when we face all the things that we have to do as a student as problems rather than opportunities. Just think about all that reading – all those lectures – gulp! It is too easy just to think of this as an imposing mountain of hard work and struggle.

Why not try to reframe your negative into a positive? Try to realise what a wonderful opportunity it is to have all this time to devote to yourself and your studies. Being a student can be the best time of your life – a time when you can think and learn, when you can make new friends and try out new opportunities. A time to flourish.

Each positive thought will make your life easier – each negative thought that you have just makes the mountain grow!

Was that instant negative thinker you? How does it make you feel? Will you try using the more positive language? When?

Start now!

Now is the time to try something different. Thus if you normally say, 'That looks really hard!' when faced with a tough assignment, try to see it as an opportunity not a problem. Try saying, 'This is an excellent module, it is really challenging – and it takes me much nearer my overall goal.' This very simple and basic re-framing stops it feeling like a burden: once this stops, you can grow with the work rather than being crushed by it.

So, from this moment forward, instead of saying 'That's hard' try saying, 'That looks really interesting!' or 'I'm really looking forward to this assignment.' And do not just try this once or twice and then give it up. Even though these positive statements may seem really strange at first, if you keep them up, you will find that they make a difference to how you feel about your work. This will then improve the work that you actually do. And, yes, this will mean that you have to start to accept a more positive you! You will have to accept a change in yourself.

● **Tip:** Do give this positive re-framing a chance to work. Try not to fear the change in yourself. Try to like the new you – it is still you!

'It's an … experience'

If problems can become opportunities, similarly disasters become fully blown learning experiences. This is a bit like the old adage, every cloud has a silver lining. Rarely is anything so bad that we cannot benefit from it in some way. Perhaps you lost your job? Surely that left you free to get a better one? Maybe you lost your home? Then there was the whole world of change and excitement open to you.

Has anything like this happened to you? How did you cope? What did you do? Hopefully, although it really felt like a disaster when it first happened – whatever it was – you did get something from it. Can you remember what that was?

So whatever happens to you as a student – see what you can learn from it:

■ Did you get a lower grade than you expected for an assignment? Spend real time trying to work out what went wrong.

■ Cannot understand the question of your latest assignment? Well, ask for help – talk it over with a study partner.

For every 'disaster' there is a lesson to be learned. Indeed we repeatedly urge you to learn from your mistakes. And an irritating but true fact is that we can actually learn much more from our mistakes than we ever can from what we just do well.

Imagine getting an excellent grade for your very first essay in a subject – but not knowing what you actually did right? This can be a very disorientating and disempowering experience. You can end up feeling more lost rather than less. But getting feedback on all the things that you did wrong in that assignment can tell you much that will help you in future assignments. Of course this will only work if you do something about it – if you look for the learning experience and try to get something from it.

Okay – I'll try that

And the choice really is yours, you can just choose to sit there and cry – and say 'If only...' or you can do something. So, instead of feeling sorry for yourself or blaming other people or just giving up when things go wrong (and things will go wrong) make the effort to analyse the situation. Find out what went wrong and notice exactly what you will have to do differently to make sure that next time it is a success.

For example, if you do get that really low grade, use all the relevant sections in this book that might help you do much better next time. In particular you might look at:

■ organisation and time management – so that you manage your time more effectively

■ creative learning – so that you develop a brainstorming technique that will really open up an assignment question – and a pattern notemaking system so that your research is more active and useful

■ QOOQRRR – so that you develop targeted research and active reading skills and hence get much more from your reading

■ the essay, report or presentation – so that you make sure you understand how to present your work most effectively.

'I have a choice'

Another really important re-framing of our vocabularies is to replace **should** with **choice**. Should is a big victim word: I should do my homework; I should visit the library... Oh and don't we feel sorry for ourselves and don't we make everyone suffer for it! Remember you always have choices, you can do your homework, visit the library ... or go to the cinema.

If you do your homework or go to the library – go with good grace and work really hard. If you go to the cinema, relax, have a good time and try not to worry about your work for one evening.

Remember that whatever we do or do not do, there is always a consequence, a price to pay. Accept that. It's just like when you choose whether or not to become a student. Either choice has a price attached.

■ If you do choose to become a student, there is a price to pay in terms of time, effort and commitment – and there are the rewards that you have decided for yourself.

■ If you choose not to become a student, there is a different sort of price to pay – you may have more time but maybe you will be stuck in a job that you do not like and which does not satisfy you.

Once you do choose to do something, accept that you have chosen to do it, accept the 'price', give 100% and do it with good grace. If you do not do it, accept that, too.

How does this sound to you? What implications does it have for you as a student? How will it change the way you behave as a student?

Changes, changes, changes

We are now moving on to consider how change for you might have an impact on those around you. We will suggest that making positive friends can help you as a student. But first let us ask you: What is your family like? How do your friends view the world at the moment? Are all the people in your world full of energy and a zest for life? Or do they all sit around feeling unmotivated and basically sorry for themselves? If it is the latter, then you will stick out like a sore thumb if you suddenly become all optimistic and positive. You will be treated rather strangely if suddenly you see opportunity everywhere instead of the problems that they all see. This can be a real challenge for the positive student of whatever age.

Young ones: Young students have peer pressure to deal with, for it is not really acceptable to be all positive and enthusiastic as a student. Everyone knows that students have to go around looking bored and suspicious all the time. Enjoying life is ridiculous and enjoying studying is just plain mad!

If everybody you know has a negative attitude to life and studying, it can be really difficult to be optimistic and positive. And it can take just too much energy to remain optimistic when all around you are miserable. Something has to give! It may be that in this company you just slip back into being negative and uncommitted yourself – and this will cost you.

Young at heart: With the more mature students, whilst on the surface it may seem okay to be a committed and motivated student, they can find that their family and friends really resent them changing. For one thing, the new positive person just feels rather strange to them. They felt more comfortable with the old negative person – they knew who that was, they knew what to expect. They do not want this person to change. It is too uncomfortable.

Another thing is that the new person has new interests and commitments. Suddenly they do not have as much time to give to their family and friends. Suddenly the family members have to help with the shopping and the cooking. Friends discover that you do not always answer the phone, you cannot go out with them three nights a week and you do not drop everything for a cup of tea whenever they feel like calling. This does not feel like a good change to them!

This student has to be very strong to keep to their commitments – and they will have to make a special effort to convince family and friends that it will all be worthwhile in the long run.

Gently does it

Now we are not suggesting that the only way to deal with negative responses from family and friends is to be confrontational – or that you ought to give them all up! Rather, we want to alert you to the fact that you may encounter resentment as you do change – and you will need tact and diplomacy to help your family and friends to travel with you. You will need to help your family and friends to accept and, hopefully, to get to like and appreciate the new you. If being the new positive student is important to you, it is important to bring your family and friends along with you. You may well encounter resistance at first – remember, they will not like change either – but if it is important to you, you have to work through this somehow.

Positive friends

Further, as we start to build ourselves up as positive people, it will help if we can make some positive friends. Positive friends can reinforce our new positive attitude; positive study partners can make the whole job of studying easier, more rewarding and much, much more enjoyable. And at a very simple level, positive people will not be using up your energy just to keep them afloat – you will be able to use your energy to progress.

> ■ **So, change for you will have an impact on those around you – how do you propose to deal with this?**

And finally...

We have already argued that adopting a positive vocabulary can make a difference to how you view the world. In this last, long, section we are going to take that one step further by exploring some other positive things to do to build self-confidence.

... even more positively

If every time you face something new that little voice in your mind seems to call out:'watch out! You'll be sorry! That's dangerous! ...', as Jeffers says, you will have to work to drown out that negative voice with a new positive one of your choosing. You have to learn to respond differently to the things that happen to you. So, instead of immediately saying things like: 'I'll never be any good at that' start saying, 'I can do it'. Wake up in the morning and let your first thought be, 'It's a great day!' Say, 'I am beautiful...I am loved...I am strong... I am a great student.' When you sit down to study do not say, 'I don't want to be here.' Or, 'I can't do this'. Say, 'This is great!' 'I'm looking forward to this topic'. Develop your own statements – the ones that make you feel good, energised and strong.

● **Tip:** Put these statements in the positive and in the present tense. So it's not, 'I will not be afraid' but, 'I am brave.' The former only emphasises the thing that you do not want to be, afraid. Putting things in the future tense always seems to put them out of reach somehow. And you want the positive energy now – not in some unrealisable future!

Don't stop

Once you start using these positive statements, it is important to keep them going. You will have had the little negative voice for a long time: when it begins to disappear – to be drowned out by the positive voice – you can get a real sense of euphoria and release. Suddenly it feels as though you don't need your positive statements any more.

But if you stop, that old negative voice will come right back. So start the positive statements – and keep them up. Every time you have a spare moment, maybe as you travel somewhere or as you tidy up, repeat your positive statements to yourself. When fear pops out, repeat your positive statements – I promise you will feel the panic subside.

Stick 'em up

Some people write their positive statements on cards and stick them round the house – by the bed, on the bathroom mirror.... You can even put a positive statement on the screen saver on your computer! (We've got 'I am powerful' on one and **joy** on another. These give a quick boost when they appear – making it easier to get back to work.) Immerse yourself in positivity as you immerse yourself in your studies.

It's win/win

We have had students feed back that positive thinking does not just help them with their studies – although it definitely does that. They also say that it has given them new confidence at work – suddenly they can speak up in meetings where ordinarily they would remain silent. They volunteer for things that they would never have dared do before. They even start to look for more challenging and rewarding jobs because now they realise they have much more ability than they had ever given themselves credit for – and they intend to use that energy to improve their whole lives.

Just do it

When you do decide on new goals for yourself, investigate what it will take to succeed – and then do it! For you will not get that new job if you do not investigate what they are looking for, and make sure that your c.v. provides this information. Neither can you sit in a corner glowing positively and expect that essay to write itself – for that really will not happen! However, you can investigate what it takes to do a good essay, and then do it.

In conclusion

So, we have looked at the academic environment briefly and argued that if you have self-confidence and self-esteem you will do better in your studies. We acknowledged that entering education – the unknown – can be fearful for everybody, and perhaps even more so for those who do not see themselves as typical students or as academics. If this is you, we recommend that you take time to actively work on this.

We explored briefly where our fears originate and we considered that they might be a legacy from evolution and a consequence of an over-protective upbringing. In either case we argued that there were steps that you can take to do something about this. We then looked in some detail at how to overcome your fears and become more positive – paying particular attention to losing the victim mentality and accepting responsibility for your own life. We argued that re-framing fear itself could help – as would adopting a positive vocabulary and making positive friends, especially a positive study partner.

Now, it is quite likely that some of this has actually made you a little more fearful in the first instance. Well, you know the answer to that – feel the fear and do it anyway! It is exciting and liberating to be in charge of your own life – enjoy your fear, it means you are still alive!

And remember, all the things that we have mentioned here have worked for all the students that have tried them out with us. You will only know if they work for you by actually trying them. So, give them a go – and once you have started, keep them going!

> **Mini-review:** As this can be an especially emotional topic we have put this little mini-review here for you. As always, reflect back over this section and make your learning conscious. What have you read? Why did you read it? How did it make you feel? What have you learned? Can you use it in your studies? How? Where? What else will you need to find out? What else will you need to do? When will this happen?

Chapter conclusion

In this chapter we have explored the human, affective, dimension of the academic environment and of being a student. We have paid particular attention to the role of fear and the benefits of positive thinking and self-confidence. We have also looked at several strategies that can help anyone build their self-confidence in any environment – especially re-framing fear, losing the victim mentality and developing a positive vocabulary.

Review points

When thinking about what you have read and the activities that you have engaged in, you might feel that you have:

■ briefly reviewed the nature of the academic environment – and reminded yourself how active you must be in learning the practices of your academic subject

■ thought about the impact of fear and a lack of self-confidence on you as a student

■ considered the origins of fear in humans – evolution and upbringing

■ explored some steps that you might take to improve your own self-confidence and assertiveness in the academic environment.

Further reading

If you want to follow up some of the ideas in this chapter, you might like to look at:
Cohen, S.B. (1997) *The Maladapted Mind* Psychology Press
Jeffers, S. (1987) *Feel the fear and do it anyway* Century, London

8 How to succeed in group work

Aims

To consider the role of group work in the academic environment – and to focus on developing group work skills.

Learning outcomes

It is intended that after reading this chapter and engaging in the activities set you will have:

- developed an awareness of the role and potential of group work in the academic environment
- engaged in activities designed to develop your group work skills.

Introduction

Group work can be one of the most emotionally charged areas of a student's life. Many students see only the problems associated with working in a group. Perhaps because they never get heard in a group, perhaps because they usually do all the work – whatever the problem, group work makes them unhappy. If you have doubts about group work or if you just want to get the most out of it, then this section is for you.

Colleges and universities are increasingly building group activities into their programmes. Some because they have an ideological commitment to collaborative learning – they believe that we are inter-dependent beings and should recognise and build on that. Others feel that group work offers support to their students – tasks are easier when they are shared. Still others feel that they are pragmatically preparing students for the world of work – for if you cannot work with other people, you are unlikely to be able to keep a job.

Whatever your college or university's reasons for asking you to engage in group work, we recommend that you try to get the most from it – and to help you, we are going to explore the what, why and how of group work. In order to do that we have drawn very heavily on the group work theories of Business – for it is in Business that group work is particularly valued.

Group work made simple: the pyramid discussion

A simple group starting activity is the pyramid discussion. When asked to start a group project:

■ think about the topic on your own

■ discuss ideas in pairs

■ build arguments in fours

■ feed back your whole group thinking in a plenary.

What is group work?

A group has to have a membership of two or more people. Typically there should be a sense of shared identity – that is, you should all have a sense that you are a group and that you have shared or common goals. Further within the group there should be a feeling of interaction and inter-dependence – a sense that you can achieve something together.

Perhaps it is in these initial definitions of a group that we have hit upon some of the problems with academic groups. How many people in an academic group do feel that sense of identity and inter-dependence? How many embrace the task and the sense of shared goals?

If this sounds like groups that you have been in – or that you are in now – what are you going to do to make your group feel and operate like a group?

Students in groups

In school, college or university there can be many forms of group work. For one thing, and as we keep reminding you, you can sort out a study partner or a study group to make study more collaborative and support-ive. You can build your own groups to share the reading for assignments, to discuss assignment questions – to proof read your work (as the tutors did in Chapter 7).

There can also be group activities organised by the tutor – from class discussions to the formal, assessed group project. Typically the best thing you can do is participate in these as positively as possible.

Academic groups

■ Class discussion or activity – based around something that has come up in a class.

■ Tutorials – two or more students meeting with a tutor and working together on a topic or task.

■ Seminars – a group of students meeting with a tutor. Typically working together on a topic covered in a lecture programme.

■ Group assignments – where students are asked to produce something collectively. For example you may have to prepare a presentation or a seminar, or write and produce a report, magazine or a video. Perhaps you will be awarded a collective grade.

● **Tips:**
● Group work is typically designed to reduce the workload whilst increasing the amount of active and interactive learning that takes place – take advantage of this.
● Sometimes the process, as well as the product, is assessed. Here, students will be asked to reflect on the whole group work process. That is, how you worked as a group – roles that were adopted – problems that occurred and how they were solved. Make notes as you go along!

Why groups?

Group work offers many advantages to students of all ages – yes, really! For one thing it offers an opportunity to share the workload. It really is easier to do all the reading for a module if you share it out. Further, group work at its best fosters active learning. You are expected to discuss things in a group – that reading for instance; in this way, everyone in the group will learn more than if they had just done something on their own. Not only this, you also get to refine your personal and inter-personal skills if you learn to discuss ideas and negotiate strategies with tact and diplomacy in your group: you do have to be assertive rather than aggressive in a group. Another advantage of group work is that a good group offers social support that can break down some of the isolation sometimes associated with being a student.

Disadvantages

Of course there can be disadvantages to group work. One disadvantage is linked to the fact that many group activities are now assessed. Students have become increasingly aware of the importance of good grades. Thus they are incredibly resentful of those in the group who do not pull their weight, who do not stay on track, who dominate or bully or distract. There can also be groups where members stay silent – or groups where the same people always speak. None of this feels satisfactory and it causes much resentment.

Resolving conflict

But every disadvantage can become an advantage if you work out how to resolve the problems that you encounter. So notice what is happening in your groups. Notice how difficult situations are resolved. Notice how unmotivated people are encouraged to give of their best... And put these notes in your *curriculum vitae* file. When you apply for a job you will be able to prove that you are good at group work by giving examples from your time at college or university. It is the examples that you give – and the way that you discuss them – that will make all the difference in that vital job interview!

And this does refer to another 'why' of group work – it can and does prepare you for your future employment.

How to 'do' group work

The best way to get the most from group work is to approach it positively, determined to get the most from it. If you really dislike group work, but have to engage in it – fake it to make it: role play being an active, positive student.

Another simple and very effective strategy is to choose your groups with care. Do not just team up with those people sitting next to you – or those nice chatty people from the canteen! Group tasks normally involve hard work: choose people who are as motivated, positive and industrious as you when you are choosing your group.

SWOT your group work

SWOT stands for Strengths, Weaknesses, Opportunities and Threats.

- What are your group work strengths?

- What are your weaknesses?

- What opportunities are there for you in group work?

- What threats?

▶

Once you have answered these questions, think about your answers – discuss them with your study partner:

■ What do they tell you about yourself?

■ What do they tell you about how you should approach group work?

A business-like approach to group work

Management theorists like Belbin and Adair (see boxes) have worked to de-mystify group work forms and processes so that businesses can run more effectively. Have a look at the information in the boxes and see what they tell you about how to make groups work. As always ask yourself, 'How will knowing this make me a more successful student?' For, in the end you must work out how knowing those things will help you to succeed in the group activities that you will be expected to undertake at college or university.

● **Tip:** If you are expected to reflect on your group work experiences – using the following information will definitely improve your grade!

Belbin's group roles

There are eight key roles that management experts like Belbin (1981) have identified in group activities. We have listed these below indicating the possible strengths and weaknesses involved:

■ *Company worker* – a dutiful, organised person, who may tend to inflexibility

■ *Chair* – a calm, open minded person, who may not shine creatively

■ *Shaper* – a dynamic person who may be impatient

■ *Creative thinker* – one who may come up with brilliant ideas, though these may be unrealistic

■ *Resource investigator* – an extrovert character who may respond well to the challenge but who may lose interest

■ *Monitor* – a sober, hard-headed individual who keeps everything on track, but who may lack inspiration

■ *Team worker* – a mild social person with plenty of team spirit – may be indecisive

■ *Completer/Finisher* – conscientious, a perfectionist, maybe a worrier.

▶

Let's pause here to go over the list.

- Which description most fits you?

- Are you happy with this?

- What are you going to do about it?

● **Tips**
● Experiment with group work. Adopt different roles in different academic groups. Each time you vary your role in a group you will develop different aspects of your personality; this is a good thing.
● Decide to use your group work experiences to develop your c.v. – and get you that job. So as you move through team worker, leader, information gatherer, creative thinker, completer, etc. make notes on your experiences for your c.v. folder.
● Whilst eight roles are indicated here, research indicates that academic groups work best if they only contain four or five people – any more and you start to get passengers.
● In a small group, allocate roles wisely, but make sure that you have a chairperson and that everyone does know what the task is, what they are doing – and when it all has to be completed.

Adair's processes

As there is theory as to the **roles** adopted in group situations, so there are arguments as to the **processes** that groups go through. Adair argues that groups have distinct forms, or pass through distinct transformations, as they encounter the task, settle down to it and finally pull it off. These are known as forming, storming, norming and performing – some people also speak of a fifth stage, mourning.

Forming is where the group comes together and takes shape. This forming period is a time of high anxiety as people work out:

- who is in the group – and what they are like

- what the assignment is – what it involves

- what the 'rules' are – about behaviour, about the task, about assessment

- what they will have to do to get the job done – and who will be doing 'all the work'.

Storming is where conflict arises as people sort out all the confusions highlighted above. This is where people seek to assert their authorities, and get challenged. Typically this is a 'black and white' phase – everything seems all

▶

good or all bad: compromise is not seen. At this stage people are reacting emotionally **against** everything as they challenge:

■ each other

■ the value of the task

■ the feasibility of the task (you cannot be serious!).

● **Tip:** If you do not like group work, ask yourself, is it because you do not like conflict? Perhaps you just find this phase uncomfortable? If this is so, remind yourself that this phase passes.

Norming, as the name suggests, is where the group begins to settle down. Here that sense of inter-dependence develops as:

■ plans are made

■ standards are laid down

■ co-operation begins

■ people are able to communicate their feelings more positively.

Performing is where the group gets on and does what it was asked to do. It is now that the task can be undertaken and completed – and success can be experienced! Here it is useful if:

■ roles are accepted and understood

■ deadlines are set and kept to

■ communication is facilitated by good inter-personal skills.

● **Tip:** Share your phone numbers and your e-mail addresses. Do have a group leader who will take responsibility for chivvying people along. Do set people tasks that they *can* do.

Mourning: The fifth stage, mourning, is supposed to follow a successful and intense group experience. As you work hard to complete an assignment with people, you develop links and bonds. Typically you enjoy the sense of mutual support and commitment. The feeling of inter-dependence is very satisfying. When all this ends as the task ends, there can be a real sense of loss.

● **Tips:**
● **Be prepared for the sense of loss.**
● **Work to keep in contact with good team players – you may be able to work with them again.**

▶

Queries:

■ Do you recognise any of these stages?

■ Now that you know about them think how you might use this knowledge to your advantage.

■ How will you draw on this information in your next group activity?

■ Make notes so that you do not forget.

And of course it can be like any other assignment!

There are many things that good groups have to do to work well, that is, for everyone involved to have a good time and for the task to be accomplished: we have referred to some of them above. Remember also to treat group work like any other assignment (see Chapter 9 – how to prepare better assignments).

How to succeed in group work

It still helps to:

1 Prepare to research: open your research folders, analyse the task, making sure that you know exactly what you have been asked to do or make – essay, report, presentations, seminar, etc. Then:

  ■ analyse the question – all of it

  ■ have the overview – and fit the task to the module learning outcomes

  ■ use creative brainstorming and notemaking strategies

  ■ action plan – work out **who** is doing what, why, where and when!

2 Follow the action plan – undertake targeted research and active reading.

3 Review your findings.

4 Plan the outline – of the report, seminar, presentation or whatever.

5 Prepare the first draft.

6 Leave a time lag.

7 Review, revise and edit – agree on a final draft.

8 Proof read – or rehearse if it involves a group presentation.

9 Hand work in on or before a deadline.

10 Review your progress!

● **Tip: If your group work review forms part of the formal assessment**:
Ask your tutor exactly what it is that they are assessing **before** you even start the
group activity. In this way you can note the relevant information as it arises and have
it there ready for when you perform your formal review of your group project.

Conclusion

We have used this section of the book to explore group work in the academic setting. We have stressed that group work can be a positive,
supportive and interactive learning experience – especially if you tackle
group activities with enthusiasm and commitment and with the co-operation of committed group members. At the same time we stressed that
you can benefit even from problem groups by noting how your problems
were overcome – and that you use such reflections in a formal group
review and in your job applications.

We stressed how an awareness of group roles and processes can help
you understand and succeed in your group activities. Finally we compared success in group assignments with success in any assignment –
making links with the ten-step plan, prepare and review strategy introduced in Chapter 9.

Good luck with your group activities. Enjoy your group work – groups
really can be supportive, exciting and productive.

Group building activities

There are management team building games that you might like to experiment
with to develop your group work skills – and for the fun of it. We have included
one below; you can search out others if you wish.

The Paper Tower

In this activity you will need to gather together some students who want to
develop their group work skills and some simple resources.

The goal will be for groups to construct a paper tower with a given supply of
resources. Variations on this include: designing, producing and testing a non-
breakable egg container or balancing a spoon on a paper tower. The egg
container is the more dramatic!

Aim

To develop group work skills through practical activity, observation and feedback.

▶

Learning outcomes

By the end of this activity participants will have developed:

■ a sense of the social support offered by group work

■ an idea of their own approach to group work

■ a sense of the fun of group work

■ an idea of the positive benefits of undertaking tasks in a team rather than alone

■ some strategies for successful group participation.

Resources

Large quantities of newspaper, cellotape, paper clips and rubber bands – sufficient for all participants.

The Paper Tower Exercise

1   Divide participants into groups of 5-6 people. Each group has to choose an observer who will not participate but who will note how the other people do so. The participants have to build a tower with the resources to hand. Each group will 'present' their tower to the other groups. Each observer will feed back how his or her group performed. (Allow 20-30 minutes tower building time.)

2   Whilst the students build their towers the observer makes notes as to the roles adopted by individual members or the processes engaged in by the group. The observer notes how people engage in the group task.

3   Groups report back on the criteria they had chosen for their tower, the tower itself – and how they felt the group performed. The observer feeds back (in constructive terms) on the roles and/or processes of the group.

4   Plenary: hold a plenary to discuss what the participants have learned from the activity – and how they will draw on this in the future.

Review points

When reviewing this activity participants might note that they:

■ enjoyed it – it was fun

■ benefited from being part of a team

■ have some idea of how they performed in a group activity

■ have learned something useful about group work that they will build on in the future.

Review points

When thinking about what you have read and the activities that you have engaged in, you might feel that you have:

☐ developed an awareness of the forms and processes of group work – so that you are in a position to make the most of group activities in the future

☐ developed an awareness of the potential of group work in the academic environment

☐ developed an awareness of how to use your group work experiences at college or university to improve your job applications.

Further reading

If you are interested in this topic you may wish to have a look at the following:

Adair, J. (1983) *Effective leadership*, (1987) *Effective team building*, (1987) *Not bosses but leaders*

Belbin (1981) *Managing teams: why they succeed or fail*, Heinemann: London

9 How to prepare better assignments

Aims

To prepare you for successful academic study by examining assessment with a special focus on developing academic communication skills and practices.

Learning outcomes

That after reading through this chapter, and engaging with the activities set, you will have:

- considered the nature of assessment and issues surrounding assessment

- considered the nature of communication and issues surrounding communicating effectively in your assignments

- considered the value of writing to learn as opposed to learning to write

- considered key academic assessment/communication forms: the essay, report, presentation and seminar

- started the process of organising yourself for successful assessment – with an emphasis on planning, preparation, practising and reviewing techniques.

- made links between assessment activities and other activities covered in this text: organisation and time management, using the overview, being creative, notemaking, targeted research and active reading.

Introduction

Assessment is one of the most potentially fraught areas in a student's life. Nobody really enjoys being assessed: it smacks of being judged, evaluated, weighed up. This means that we can fail, we can make mistakes – mistakes that reveal us to be foolish or inadequate.

Funnily enough, that is not really the point of assessment! In this chapter we are going to examine the nature of assessment – why do we have to be assessed? What is the point of it all? We will move on to consider the communication aspects of assessment – for if we can communicate our ideas effectively we will do better in our assignments. We will then move on to explore how to successfully plan, prepare and practise some of the major assessment modes: the essay, report, presentation and seminar. Examinations were covered in Chapter 5 – how to pass exams.

Assessment

Assessment is part of a measurable education system. If we have a system that is going to offer credits, certificates and other qualifications, we will also have assessment.

It can help if you view assessment in a more positive light. Try to see assessment as a chance to:

- learn your material

- show what you know.

And remember, assessment is not a trick – you will be assessed on material that you have covered on a programme of study.

Formative and summative

In the education system we often talk of formative and summative assessment. **Formative** is developmental – it is intended to measure a student's progress at a particular moment in a subject. With formative assessment there should be an emphasis on tutor feedback, and that feedback is designed to help you do better in the summative assessment. **Summative** assessment usually occurs at the end of a programme of study and it is designed to measure the student's overall achievement in the unit, course or programme.

Arguably the best forms of assessment manage to bring about learning in the student as they engage in the assessment process. That is, that whilst there is a product – the essay, report or presentation – that can be assessed, preparing and putting together the product is a learning process.

Activity: Thinking about assessment

Think of some assessment tasks that you have had to engage with in the past. What did you think of them? Make a few quick notes.

Here are some points gained from other students:

▓ Exams – and there are lots of different types of these – from the multiple choice, to the essay answer. I really like exams – they give me a chance to show off – but I know other students who hate them!

▓ Well, there was my driving test. I did all right – but the new written test must be a bit difficult for those who do not feel confident with their reading skills.

▓ Coursework – I hate exams so I chose a course that was assessed only on coursework. That suited me! At the same time, there are people who hate coursework the same way that I hate exams. They feel that this just means they are being judged all the time, across a whole course – rather than just at the end – and this increases their stress.

▓ My new course has set us presentations – we are going to have to get up and speak in front of the whole class! Can you imagine that?

Commentary: As always, we get back to the point that there is no one correct response to the different sorts of assessment activities that operate – exams, coursework, presentations… The trick is to discover the types of assessment you prefer and try to pick courses that use those methods. At the same time, everyone can get better at the different assessment forms – with understanding and practice – and that is what this chapter is all about.

Communication

Many people might wonder why there is a section on communication in a chapter on assessment. Maybe that is the problem: when we are preparing an essay or getting that presentation ready – we are so aware of being assessed that we often forget that someone will have to read and understand the essay – that people will have to listen to, and follow, that presentation.

We have discovered that understanding what facilitates communication can help you to produce better assignments. We will be referring to that in the sections below, particularly:

■ on essay writing – look out for 'the paragraph questions'

■ on report writing – look for the sections on 'the reader'

■ on presentations – look for information on the audience, body language and the use of prompts rather than scripts.

The academic forms

In this section we are going to explore the major ways of communicating in terms of:

- **What:** the formal conventions of assessment: essay, report, presentation, seminar. Knowing what these things actually **are** can remove the unnecessary worry – have I got this right? Is this what they are after? This allows you to be concerned about the real issues – what should go in my assignment? What will I have to do, what will I have to research, to construct a good assignment? When will I do these things?

- **Why:** the particular purpose of each activity – that is, we will explore what **you** can get out of doing each particular assessment activity. If you can accept why you have to do something, you can often do it with better grace. This is a really simple way of getting better grades!

- **How:** successful planning and researching techniques – that will draw on the strategies and techniques introduced elsewhere in this book.

How to prepare better essays

What is an essay?

The word 'essay' comes from the Latin word *exagium*, which means the presentation of a case. So when constructing an essay you have to think of making a case, building a case. In some ways it can be compared with a lawyer prosecuting or defending a client.

It is not enough for the defence to say, 'He didn't do it, your honour!' The defence has to construct a case to prove that the client did not do 'it'. To do this the defence has to search for and gather the evidence to prove his/her case. The defence also has to anticipate the prosecution's evidence against the defendant. The defence has to then make the case for the defence in a series of arguments – presented one at a time. Each argument is supported by evidence. (See also Figure 9.1 and 'what is an essay' box).

The essay – legal precedent

'The defence will prove that the case against our client is utterly mistaken. In particular we will prove that he could not have been identified as being at the scene of the crime for it was too dark to make a definite identification. We will tell you that the so-called witness suffers from poor vision and therefore could not identify our client. Finally we will conclusively prove that our client was somewhere

▶

else at the time. **(Do you see how all the points have been separated out? And how they are all flagged up here in the introduction? The listeners are not left wondering, 'Where is all this going?' This is the same in an essay – and with an essay introduction.)**

1   The alley was too dark blah blah

2   The witness was not wearing his glasses blah blah

3   My client has an alibi for the time blah blah

In conclusion, we argue that despite everything that the prosecution has said, you must find our client innocent because we have conclusively proven his innocence. He definitely could not have been identified as being at the scene of the crime. Firstly it was too dark to positively identify anyone, further the witness was too short sighted to have any value placed upon his testimony and finally we proved beyond a shadow of a doubt that our client was somewhere else at the time of the incident.' **(Here in the conclusion all the main arguments are re-visited, all the main points are re-stated.)**

● **Tip:** See Figure 9.1 The essay structure diagram.

One step at a time

When it comes to searching for the answer to academic essay questions, you too – as with the legal precedent – will have to:

■ break the whole question down into mini-points that can be covered one at a time

■ search for evidence – things that other people have written – for and against your arguments

■ think of a case that you want to make

■ think of the separate arguments that would go to making your case

■ make sure you have evidence for each argument.

And you would have to do this within the academic 'rules' of your subject – that is the arguments you construct must build upon and use the arguments and evidence that already exist in your subject. So you will have to:

■ re-read your lecture or class notes to get a starting point for your research

■ read further – read around the topics looking for 'evidence'

■ present your arguments in the correct way for your subject.

Essay tips

- An essay is a continuous piece of writing. This means that it is not divided up by headings or strap headlines. These are okay in reports but not usually in essays.

- Set length: you will be told how many words to write. That is what you should write. You may be allowed your word limit plus or minus ten per cent but that is all. Any more or less and you could fail. The challenge is always to answer the question in the word limit set.

- Presentation counts. Your essay must look professional and well cared for – preferably word-processed. It must not look as if the dog has dribbled on it.

- Be formal: use formal English – and do not abbreviate.

- Give us some space! Essays have to be marked – double line space, leave a margin and write on one side of the paper only – this leaves space for the marker. Typically it is the correct way to present work at university.

● **Tip:** This will only look strange to you the first few times that you do it. Then it will become perfectly normal and other ways of presenting work will look strange. Remember that uncomfortable feelings do pass.

More tips:

- get a computer
- learn to touch type
- use the Format button: format leads you to **Font and Paragraph:**
- **Font:** think about:
- font type: Arial is nice and clean, Times New Roman is the font used in academic books and journals
- font size – 10, 11 and 12 are good readable font sizes

THIS IS AN 'ARIAL' TYPE FONT, SIZE 12

THIS IS A 'TIMES NEW ROMAN' TYPE FONT, SIZE 14

THIS IS A 'GARAMOND' TYPE FONT, SIZE 16

THIS IS A 'COURIER NEW' TYPE FONT, SIZE 18

> – **Paragraph:** think about:
>
> – left align or justified
>
> – spacing – typically 1.5 or double line

Why write essays?

There are many reasons for tutors setting essays. Firstly, yes, it is a form of assessment, one that is popular with tutors. With an essay they get a piece of your work that is concrete and real – it exists. Further, once they have given it a mark they have the evidence, your work, to prove their marking was correct.

Also, it has taken you time to write an essay and it will take your tutor time to mark it. Thus it is substantial and worthy of respect.

Furthermore, the essay enables a dialogue between student and tutor. In a way, your essay is your feedback to them about what you learned from the course – and when they mark your work they can give you feedback about your writing and the understanding of the topic that you demonstrated in your essay. Make use of this feedback – ask yourself what it tells you about your understanding of the topic and your ability to communicate effectively in writing.

Write to learn

But more than this, it is intended that the process of preparing an essay is heuristic – it brings about powerful active learning. That is, as you get to grips with a question, you will revise your course material so that you develop a better understanding of it – and you will research the topic further so that you extend your knowledge.

As you study you will discover a whole range of differing arguments and opinions. When you think about all the different data, you work to synthesise what you have learned – you struggle to understand. As you then shape your data to answer a specific question, you will find that you are now struggling to communicate effectively. These are the academic practices of a successful student.

It is in the 'struggle to write' that your learning is refined. And we do mean struggle! As the typical writer says, 'Writing is easy – you just sit and stare at a blank piece of paper till your eyeballs bleed!'

Writing is hard for everyone! Not just you – or us! Once you accept that, you realise that writing is difficult because it is difficult. There does not have to be anything wrong with you!

However, there are some successful planning and preparation strategies that can help – and that is what we are going to look at now. It is here that much of the advice that we have given elsewhere in this book comes together.

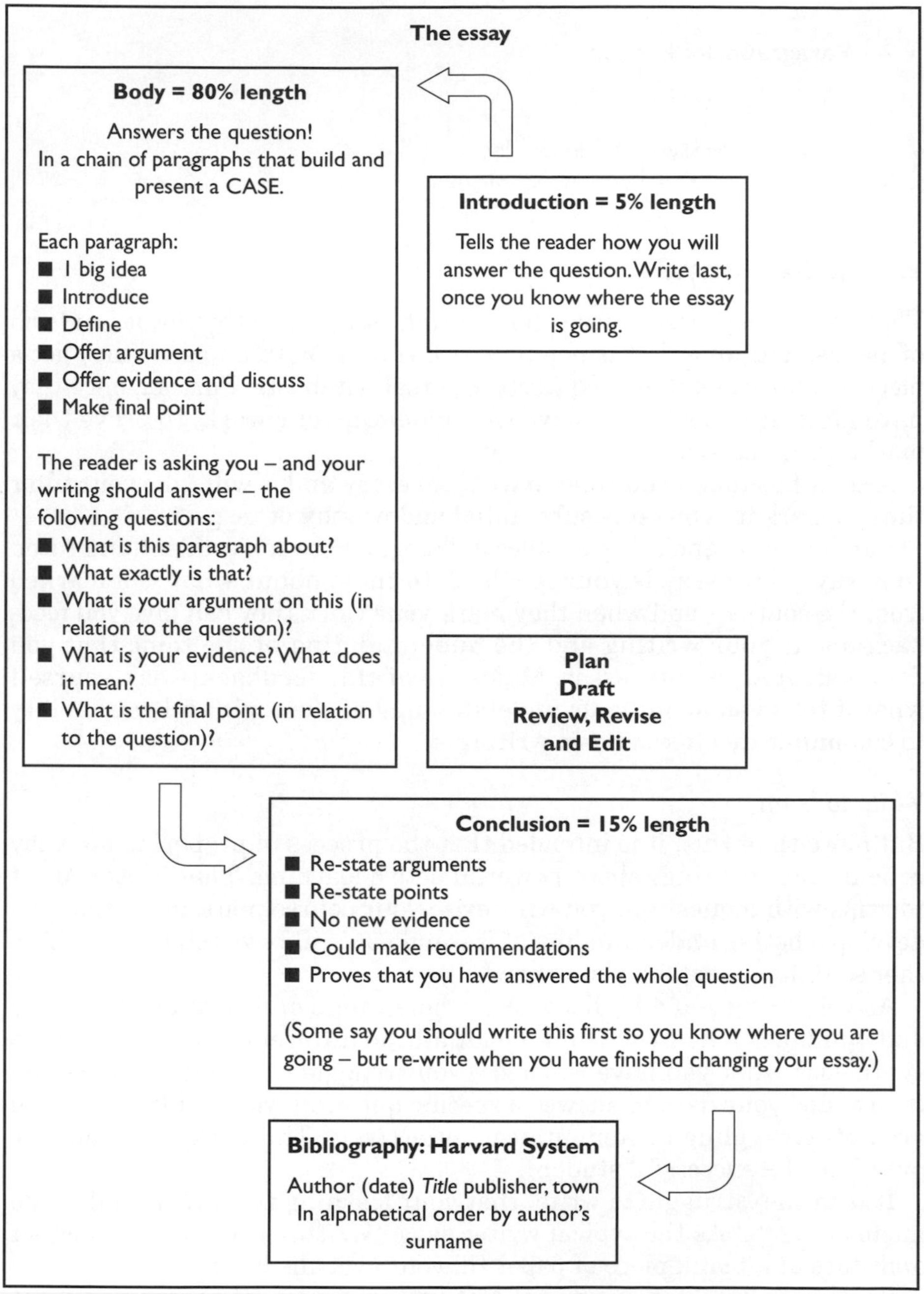

The essay

Body = 80% length

Answers the question!
In a chain of paragraphs that build and present a CASE.

Each paragraph:
■ I big idea
■ Introduce
■ Define
■ Offer argument
■ Offer evidence and discuss
■ Make final point

The reader is asking you – and your writing should answer – the following questions:
■ What is this paragraph about?
■ What exactly is that?
■ What is your argument on this (in relation to the question)?
■ What is your evidence? What does it mean?
■ What is the final point (in relation to the question)?

Introduction = 5% length

Tells the reader how you will answer the question. Write last, once you know where the essay is going.

**Plan
Draft
Review, Revise
and Edit**

Conclusion = 15% length
■ Re-state arguments
■ Re-state points
■ No new evidence
■ Could make recommendations
■ Proves that you have answered the whole question

(Some say you should write this first so you know where you are going – but re-write when you have finished changing your essay.)

Bibliography: Harvard System

Author (date) *Title* publisher, town
In alphabetical order by author's surname

Figure 9.1 The essay structure

What is an essay?

An essay has a formal convention – a set style to which it must conform or it is not an essay. The convention is as follows:

The body

This is the section of the essay where you do answer the question that you have been set. It can be 80% of total length. You answer the question in a chain of paragraphs that you have organised to build a well-argued case. **Note:** Typically written in the third person, past tense. That is: *It can be argued that* rather than *I think this…*

Paragraph structure

Each paragraph also has a set convention: introduction; definition; argument; evidence plus discussion; final point. This is where it is useful to remember that you are communicating with a **reader**! When writing imagine your reader asking you questions – and make sure that your writing answers them.

Paragraph as dialogue:

- *What is this paragraph about?*
  Introduce your topic

- *What exactly is that?*
  Define, explain or clarify

- *What is your argument – in relation to the question?*
  Say something about your topic

- *What is your evidence? What does it mean?*
  Say who or what supports your argument. Give evidence. Say what the evidence means.

- *What is your final point? (How does this paragraph relate to the question as a whole?)*
  Take the paragraph back to the question.

Sometimes your writing has to acknowledge contradictory evidence (the people that disagree with you) as you go – here are some questions to encourage you to address those.

The advanced paragraph questions:

- What is this paragraph about?

- What exactly is that?

- What is your argument – in relation to the question?

- What is your evidence? What does it mean? That is:

▶

Who or what supports this view? What is the evidence? What does it mean? What is the opposing evidence? What does that mean? Therefore…?

■ What is your final point? (How does this paragraph relate to the question as a whole?)

(Again, whilst these questions address *you* – you write in the third person, past tense.)

● **Tip:** Write these questions out on an index card and stick them on your computer screen. Look at them when you write.

The introduction

This is the first paragraph of the essay. It can be between five and seven per cent of total length (do the maths!). In the introduction you tell the reader how you are going to answer the question. Typically you write some introductory remarks that acknowledge the importance of the topic – and then give the **agenda** of the essay.

● **Tip:** Write the introduction last, when you know where the essay is going! Writing it too soon will give you a writing block.

The conclusion

This is the last, often long, paragraph of the essay. It can be 13-15% of length. In the conclusion you re-state your main arguments and points in a way that proves that you have answered the whole question. You do not include new information or evidence, but you may make recommendations if appropriate.

● **Tip:** Use the words from the question in your conclusion to prove that you have answered the whole question.

Bibliography

Literally a book list, it is now a record of all the sources you have used to construct your essay.

● **Tips**
  ● Harvard System: author, date, *Title*, publisher, town
  ● British Standard System: author, *Title*, publisher, date
  ● Alphabetical order by author's surname.
  ● These days you may be citing [quoting or referring to] material from lectures, television, film video and the Internet and you need to record your sources in the same format as with written texts.

Internet referencing tips

Documents obtained from the Internet:

All references begin with the same information that would be provided for a printed source (or as much of that information as possible): author (date) Title publisher. The WWW information is then placed at the end of the reference.

Note: It is important to give the date of access because documents on the Web may change in content, move, or be removed from a site all together.

For example:

▨ *An article*:
Jacobson, J.W., Mulick, J.A., Schwartz, A.A (1995). A history of facilitated communication: Science, pseudoscience, and antiscience: Science working group on facilitated communication. *American Psychologist*, 50, 750-765. Retrieved 25 January 1996, from http://www.apa.org/journals/jacobson.html

▨ *A newspaper article*:
Sleek, S. (1996, January). Psychologists build a culture of peace. APA Monitor, pp. 1, 33 [Newspaper, selected stories on-line]. Retrieved 25 January 1996, from http://www.apa.org/monitor/peacea.html

▨ *WWW document*:
Li, X. and Crane, N. (1996, 20 May). Bibliographic formats for citing electronic information. Retrieved 10 March 1997, from
http://www.uvm.edu/~xli/reference/estyles.html

▨ *WWW document – corporate author*:
American Psychological Association (1996). How to cite information from the World Wide Web. Retrieved 17 March 1997, from
http://www.apa.org/journals/webref.html

▨ *WWW document – no author*:
A field guide to sources on, about and on the Internet: Citation formats. (1995, Dec 18). Retrieved 7 February 1996, from
http://www.cc.emory.edu/WHSCL/citation.formats.html

▨ *WWW document – no author, no date*:
GVU'S 8th WWW user survey. (n.d.). Retrieved 8 August 2000, from
http://www.cc.gatech.edu/gvu/usersurveys/survey1997-10/

▨ *An abstract*:
Rosenthal, R.(1995). State of New Jersey v. Margaret Kelly Michaels: An overview [Abstract]. *Psychology, Public Policy, and Law*, 1, 247–271. Retrieved 25 January 1996, from http://www.apa.org/journals/ab1.html

▶

Film/video:

Maas, J.B. (Producer), and Gluck, D.H. (Director). (1979). Deeper into hypnosis [Film]. Englewood Cliffs, NJ: Prentice Hall.

CD ROMS:

Newspaper or magazine on CD-ROM:
Gardner, H. (1981, December). Do babies sing a universal song? *Psychology Today* [CD-ROM], pp. 70–76

Abstract on CD-ROM:
Meyer, A.S. and Bock, K. (1992). The tip-of-the-tongue phenomenon: Blocking or partial activation? [CD-ROM]. *Memory Cognition*, 20, 715–726. Abstract from: SilverPlatter File: PsycLIT Item: 80-16351

Article from CD-ROM Encyclopedia:
Crime. (1996). In Microsoft Encarta 1996 Encyclopedia [CD-ROM]. Redmond, WA: Microsoft Corporation.

Dictionary on CD-ROM:
Oxford English dictionary computer file: On compact disc (2nd ed.) [CD-ROM]. (1992). Oxford: Oxford University Press.

Taken from: www.UEFAP.COM *(writing/references)*

How to prepare and write an essay

So, now that we have looked at the what and the why of the essay, we can move on to give you practical advice on how to prepare and write an essay. We are going to consider everything from examining the question and preparing to research to using your tutor's feedback effectively. We have broken this down to ten key steps.

Step 1: Prepare to research

This is the longest section – and that reflects how important good preparation is. Prepare well and you can write a good essay. Rush in to writing and you invariably miss things out and get things wrong.

It takes time

This is where it is important to manage your time (Chapter 2), for it takes a significant amount of time to prepare a good assignment. Start to work on an assignment as soon as possible. Allow several weeks to research and gather information – and leave several more weeks to drafting and re-drafting your work.

Open a research folder

It is useful to have a folder for every assignment that you are doing. The folder becomes the place where you automatically put useful notes, press cuttings, thoughts and feelings on the assignment. Without a folder, your information can drift – and your thinking will too.

Open a research folder early and start collecting information from week one of your course.

The research folder itself can be simple or elaborate – you can re-cycle old A4 envelopes or buy something really swish and attractive that will inspire you just by looking at it. The point is to open the folder so that you focus on the question early, and gather information throughout a programme of study – not in the couple of days before the deadline!

Look at the question!

Write the whole question on the outside of the folder or envelope. Do not abbreviate: if you do not write a bit of the question you will definitely not write an important part of the answer. When this happens you are throwing marks away.

Examine the question: once you have written out the question (essay titles are often called questions, even when not phrased as such), analyse every word in it. Make sure that you understand exactly what and exactly how much the question is asking you to do.

Doing this early in a course of study tunes your brain into the course itself more effectively. In this way you 'hear' more in class and 'see' more in set texts; also you may hear and see more as you read the papers and watch television! Note what you see and hear – put the notes in your research folder. This will give you more over all.

Each time you hear something in class or read something related to the topic and then put the notes that you make in your envelope, remember to write the source – author, date, title, publisher... – on the outside of the envelope and you will build up your bibliography as you go.

● **Tips**
● It sometimes helps to put the question in your own words and say it back to another student or a tutor.
● Underline every important word in the question. Then go back and underline some more words. Investigate every word underlined.
● Every word in a question is a gift – use them all. Each one is there to be investigated, questioned, challenged, argued for or against.
● Make sure that you do something about every word – don't leave any out.

Be creative

Consider every word in the question in a flexible, creative way. Don't forget to brainstorm and question matrix every word in the question (see Chapter 6).

Performing a creative loosening up activity like this allows you to cover the question in more depth and breadth. It should also reassure you – you do not need to know the answer when you look at a question but you should know how to devise more questions.

Use the overview

Cross-reference the question with the aims and learning outcomes (see Chapter 4). Remember that when answering an assignment question one brief comes from the question itself – the wider brief comes from the course, module, programme or unit that set the question.

You must be very clear about the module aims and outcomes when researching and drafting your essay. You must shape your essay so that it answers the question – and also so that it demonstrates that you have met the learning outcomes (see example in Chapter 4).

Action plan

In the light of your brainstorming and other thinking, you then have to decide exactly what you will have to do to research and produce your assignment.

Things to consider include:

■ What do you now have to do?

■ Who will you speak to (tutor, study partner, subject librarian…)?

■ What will you read?

■ When will you do these things?

● **Tip:** It helps if you draw up a detailed and systematic list of everything that you will need to do and when you will do it. Allow a column for ticking off items as you complete them (see Figure 9.2).

WHAT	WHY	WHERE	WHEN	CHECK
Note what you will research	Remind yourself *why* you are researching that topic	Note where you will look for the information	Set a date and keep to it	Check when you have done it
e.g. Key word from the assignment	e.g. It could be a word from the question *or* it could refer to a learning outcome.	e.g. Lecture notes, books, journals, etc.		
Research: Active learning	Part of question	Essential study skills Chap ……	Thursday afternoon	

Figure 9.2 A sample action plan

A typical action plan might contain:

- Which lecture notes to re-read

- Which set texts to read

- Which additional texts you would utilise

- Dates

- Check off.

Step 2: Follow the action plan: systematic and targeted research and active reading using the QOOQRRR system

Follow the plan

Once you have devised your action plan, follow it through. Read actively and interactively, using your QOOQRRR technique (see Chapter 3). Remember to get physical with the texts – mark them up, annotate, make comments and cross-references as you go – you will get much more from your reading when you do this.

Read with a purpose

Don't forget that when you are reading you are looking for the answers to the questions generated by your question matrix. Typically you are looking for them one at a time – you are not looking for the whole answer to the question in any one piece of reading. Remember the legal precedent – one point at a time!

Creative notes

Remember to make your creative pattern notes (see Chapter 6) on one side of the paper only: you do not want half of your information facing the table – you want it all facing you.

Big notes

Get really large sheets of paper – A1 rather than A4 – put a key word from the question in the centre of each sheet.

Put the notes from **all** your reading about one topic onto one sheet of paper – this becomes a potential paragraph.

Put all the evidence on another paragraph topic on another sheet of paper...

Keep going till you have all the question words covered!

Remember to put Author (date) *Title*, publisher, town – and page numbers – in your notes!

Step 3: Review your notes

Remove your notes from your research folder and lay them out in front of you. Look at what you have gathered for each paragraph. For each paragraph, consider all the 'agreeing' points and all the 'disagreeing' points. Read them again. Reflect on what you have discovered – given all this information, what do you now think? Why?

● **Tips:**
● **Notice** the evidence for and against your topic.
● **Think** what your argument will be – given the evidence.
● **Discuss your evidence!** Remember, when other people write, they are not answering your essay question. When you lasso their points, you will have to work on them to build them into your essay. This is why we always have to discuss our quotes. Relate the quote to your argument; relate it to the essay question.
● **Index surf** to brush up your paragraphs. Once you have completed your major research, and you are happy with it, you can just index surf to get little extra bits and pieces to take your work that little bit further.

Step 4: Plan

When you are ready, plan the **body** of your essay. Think of the different ideas that will go to answer the whole question. Think about building the logical case of your essay and all the different ideas that you will have to cover to answer the whole question.

Always remember that it is one main idea per paragraph. For each idea, think of a possible argument and think of the evidence that will support that argument.

Remember that your reader will be thinking of the opposite evidence – just as the prosecuting lawyer would be doing in court. So, do not just ignore inconvenient or contradictory evidence – know what it is and argue against it.

Once all the ideas are jotted down you can examine them again and number them according to where they should come in the body of your essay – order them so that you are **building** a logical case.

● **Tip:** Write all the ideas on separate pieces of paper. Move the pieces of paper around to discover the best structure for the essay.

Step 5: Write the first draft

Once you have the points (paragraph outlines) in a rough order – write the essay. Use the paragraph questions to prompt your writing:

■ What is this about?

■ What exactly is that?

■ What is your argument?

- What is the evidence? What does it mean?
- What is the opposing evidence? What does that mean?
- Therefore…?
- What is your final point?

At the end of each paragraph, remember to tie what you have written to the essay question. It is not down to your reader to guess what you are trying to say – or to think 'I wonder how this relates to the question?' If your reader has to do that then something is missing from your essay.

Intros and outros

If you write your introduction and conclusion at your first draft stage, remember that the introduction has to set the reader up to understand how the essay will answer the question. Therefore an introduction can have some general remarks about the question – how important it is, how it touches upon key issues – but you must also give the agenda of the essay, that is, the order in which you will be presenting your points. In the conclusion you must re-state your main arguments and the points that you made.

But do, do remember to change these draft intros and outros… Your whole essay should change as you review, revise and edit your work – don't lose marks by forgetting to change the introduction and conclusion!

Go with the flow

As you write your first draft, try to build a flow in your writing – remember it is a first draft and does not have to be perfect. If you try to be perfect you will hit your writing blocks.

So, when writing your first draft, do not try to answer **all** the paragraph questions the first go through. Leave gaps. Repeat yourself. Put in rough words rather than the 'best' words. Write messy sentences in poor English with no verbs. Write overlong sentences that hide the point you are trying to make. **But remember also that you will be going back over this first draft!**

First draft tips

- You are not looking for the one right answer that already exists – there are usually several ways of tackling a question. As long as you were creative with the whole question – and you cross-referenced with course aims and outcomes – you are probably on the right track.

- Write the first draft, following the plan.

▶

- Or – write your 'favourite' paragraph first to get you started.

- Do **not** even try for perfection – this **will** cause writing blocks!

- Be boring, repeat yourself – and, most importantly of all, leave gaps.

- When you get stuck for an idea put … (dot, dot, dot – this is an ellipsis) and write on.

- Academic writing is always tentative rather than definite. You will get very familiar with: **typically, it could be argued that, thus this makes a case for…**

- It can be difficult to be tentative when you do care passionately about what you are writing! Practise.

- If you write the first draft straight onto your computer, it is easier to revise and edit.

- As you play with the ideas – and possibly re-arrange them – you will need to re-write your introduction and conclusion to reflect the changes that you make; that is why it is good to leave these till last.

- Use the paragraph questions.

- At the end of each paragraph, remember to make a point. Tell the reader what you have demonstrated or proven.

- Remember to tie what you have written to the essay question. (If your reader could say, 'So?' or 'So what?' after reading your paragraph – you have not said enough.)

Step 6: Leave it!

Once you have written the first draft you feel great, the essay is great, your friends are great and life is great. Do not believe this! Put the work to one side and leave it for a while.

This will give you some distance and objectivity, but more than this: your unconscious mind will seek to close the gaps that you left.

In earlier chapters we pointed out that we do have to train our brains to remember and learn the things that we want remembered and learned – but we also have to train ourselves to work with the way that our brains actually work. Typically the brain likes closure. The brain will not be happy with all the gaps in your essay. Thus your brain will struggle to close the gaps that you have left. If you allow a break in your essay writing process you are allowing the brain to close the gaps – you are working with your brain.

Step 7: Review, revise and edit

This is the stage where you go back over your work and struggle to make it the very best it can be. Here you have to re-read what you have written – and change it. Sometimes we have to change everything – and nothing of our first draft gets left. This does not matter. Remember we are writing to learn, so our thoughts should change as we write. Also, we would never get to a good version if we did not go through our rough versions. So always be prepared to draft and re-draft your work: not only is it impossible to hit perfection on a first draft, you should not even try – it is bad technique and it can actually stop you writing anything!

■ Remember – once you have written something you have something to change but a blank page stays a blank page for an awfully long time!

On your first review, you might start from the beginning of the essay and polish as you go. After that, try to concentrate on one paragraph at a time – not necessarily in the order that the essay is written but in any order. Polishing one paragraph at a time is much better than always going back to the start. If you always go back to the beginning, you may never polish the end of the essay – and you can quickly become very bored with what you are doing.

● **Tips:**
● Review, revise and edit – this *is* the essay writing process!
● Allow plenty of time for this process.
● Go through the whole essay when doing the first and last drafts – but in between, attack one paragraph at a time.
● This is where you go back and put in the 'best' word. This is where you put in the verbs. This is where you shorten long sentences so that you make clear, effective points.
● When you have finished polishing paragraphs, check the 'links' between paragraphs – make sure that they still connect with each other.

Essay checklist

For every essay check:

■ Have you addressed the whole question?

■ Have you addressed the aims and learning outcomes?

■ Is there an introduction that gives the agenda of the essay?

■ Would that agenda actually answer the question set?

■ Are the paragraphs in the best possible order?

● **Tip:** Print off a copy of your essay. Cut up the paragraphs, mix them up, and put them in the best order.

▶

▨ Does each paragraph have its own introduction, definition, argument, evidence, and final point? Double check that you have **discussed** your evidence!

▨ Is there a conclusion re-stating the main arguments and points? Do you use all the words from the question to prove that you have answered the whole question?

▨ Is there a comprehensive bibliography (referring to every source you have mentioned in the essay)? Is it in alphabetical order by author's surname?

▨ If anything is missing or imperfect – change it.

● **Tips:**
● Allow some time for this to make sure you have written a good essay that does indeed answer the whole question.
● Use a computer.

Step 8: Proof read

Once you are happy with your essay, you are ready to stop revising it – you are ready to say, 'This is the best I can do'. At this point you still have to proof read the final version. (Sometimes we are never really 'happy' with our work, but there still comes a time to stop and move on to the next task.)

Proof reading is not editing. At this stage you are not looking to change what you have written, here you are going through looking for mistakes, grammatical errors, tense problems, spelling mistakes or typographical errors.

Note: You now know that when writing, it is useful to leave gaps knowing that the brain likes closure – it will work to fill the gaps. This works against us when we are proof reading! The brain still likes closure – this means that our eyes will 'see' what should be there rather than what is there! To get over this we have to make our proof reading 'strange'.

● **Tips:**
● Read your essay aloud.
● Swap essays with a friend – proof read each other's work.
● Cover the essay with paper and proof read one sentence at a time.
● Proof read from back to front.
● Proof read from the bottom of the page to the top.
● Proof read several times, just checking for one of 'your' mistakes at a time.
● Like everything else we do, proof reading gets better with practice.

Step 9: Hand it in

You should now be ready to hand your work in – on or before the deadline! (And remember that deadline. On most university programmes a late essay is awarded an automatic fail! This is serious.)

So once your essay is done – congratulations – but before you rush off and celebrate: remember to always keep copies of your essay. Never hand in the only copy.

Obviously if you are writing on a computer it is okay – save your work to the hard drive and to a floppy disk or two.

If writing by hand – still photocopy that essay. And if the assessment unit loses your essay, do not hand in your last copy – photocopy that! A student of ours came back and told us that the assessment unit lost her essay – the same one – three times!

Step 10: Getting work back

Typically when we get work back, we look at the grade, feel really happy or really unhappy, throw the work to one side and forget all about it. This is not a good idea. What is a good idea is to review what you have written, and see if you still think it is good. As an active learner, you should try to take control of your own criticism – you have to learn how to judge your own work, do not just rely on the tutor's opinions.

At the same time, you should also utilise the feedback that you get from the tutor – be prepared to use that feedback to write a better essay next time. So a good thing to do is to perform a SWOT analysis of our own work, that is, look for the:

Strengths

Weaknesses

Opportunities

Threats.

When you SWOT your work – look for the things that you think you did well or not so well. Then look for the things that the tutor appears to be telling you that you did well or not so well. Resolve to do something about your strengths and your weaknesses.

SWOTting your essay

Strengths – Go through the essay very carefully, look at all the ticks and positive comments. These indicate that you have done something well. Note the good things you have done – make a note to do them again.

Weaknesses – Look at all the passages without ticks or with comments suggesting that something is missing or incorrect. Note these: make a note to do something about them. Go and find the missing information – correct errors.

Opportunities – Think what you can do now to learn the subject better or improve your grades. Think how to write a better essay in your next module.

Threats – Ask yourself if anything is stopping you from doing better work. Find out what it is and do something about it. (Sometimes we can be frightened of success just as much as of failure – is this you? What are you going to do about it?)

● **Tips:**
● If you can answer an exam question on a topic previously covered in an assignment, put the assignment in your revision folder.
● If you improve the essay then the exam answer will be even better. This is a good thing.
● Share it! Read each other's work, discover different writing styles and other ways to answer a question – this stretches our thinking.

Conclusion – the essay

So, we have considered the what, why and how of the essay. With 'what' we paid attention to getting the shape of the essay right – and to building a logical case using argument and evidence. We mentioned that each subject will have its own way of presenting information and encouraged you to discover what that is for your subject (read the journals – see how the text books do it). With 'why', we emphasised that the 'struggle to write' is a learning process – we really do write to learn rather than learn to write! With 'how' we looked at an effective plan, prepare and review strategy that draws on the various techniques recommended throughout the book (and which would thus help with all our academic tasks, not just the essay). We stressed giving sufficient time to assignments, opening research folders and tying our understanding of the question to our overview of the module – using the learning outcomes to inform our research and our writing. We emphasised creativity – using brainstorming and matrixing techniques on the question itself and pattern notes to collect our data. We moved on to detail a systematic and logical system for the research, planning, writing and editing procedures; concluding with an emphasis on critical review as part of our personal development process. We hope that you now feel in a better position to approach your assignment essays.

Essay development activities

▪ **Group writing:** form a group with some friends that you trust. Brainstorm and plan 'perfect' answers to your essays. This is especially useful when preparing for exams.

▪ **Practise brainstorming:** sit down with a list of essay questions. Give yourselves ten minutes to brainstorm and plan each essay answer. Remember – brainstorming and planning get quicker with practice.

▪ **Write those paragraphs:** once you have an essay plan – sit down and use the paragraph questions to prompt your paragraph writing.

▪ **Do not aim for perfection:** get something written – change it.

▪ **Practise writing:** do not just write for assessment – get into the habit of writing something every week, even every day.

● **Tips:**
● Writing and planning both get easier with practice.
● Practise planning a letter to a friend before you write.
● Write a lot!

How to prepare better reports

Report writing is becoming an increasingly popular academic assessment activity. Superficially students often appear more familiar with the academic report; many of them will have, incorrectly, used headlines and strap headlines in their academic essays. However, typically, most students will benefit from a proper introduction to report writing – just as to all other academic conventions. In this section we will be looking at the what, why and how of reports. We will also be referring you back to the **how** of the essay – for that basic ten-step programme is a successful plan, prepare and review strategy that will work with all your assignments. What we will be trying to do here is make conscious the links that the report has with other academic forms and processes – and also to identify the things that are specific to the particular form of the report.

Reports

Reports are very popular on both Business and Science courses, further, the **project write up**, the **dissertation structure** and the **journal article** are very similar to the report, whatever your subject.

Big tip

Read the journals for your subject. Note the way they structure arguments, the way that they use evidence, and the layout and style of their articles. This will tell you how to structure arguments and present evidence in your subject – it will also be the report model that you ought to follow.

What is a report?

The essence of the report is that it is a document designed to deal with the real world – specifically, a report is a practical document that describes, details or analyses a situation in the real world such that the reader can make decisions or take specific actions. When thinking about academic reports it can be helpful to think about other reports that we might have dealt with in our lives – as long as we remember to use the proper academic and subject conventions when we come to write our reports.

Activity: Thinking about reports

Have you ever had a school report? What about a surveyor's report? Or have you read a *Which* report? What do they have in common?

Discussion: one thing that all these reports have in common is that they are designed to give specific information to specific readers. Each writer of a report knows who the readers are. Further, they will know what they expect the reader to do after they have read the report.

School report – allows the child's carer to understand how the child is doing at school. The carer can use the information to judge whether or not the child is progressing as they think they should. They can then take action if they wish.

Surveyor's report – for the potential homebuyer. Gives factual information on the status of a property. The buyer can then decide on purchase depending on the risks that they are prepared to take judged against the information that they have been given.

Which report – for a readership typically interested in purchasing something. Information given allows readers to judge different items against disclosed criteria – they can then decide on what to do depending on their own criteria for action.

Final question: how will knowing this help you to write better reports?

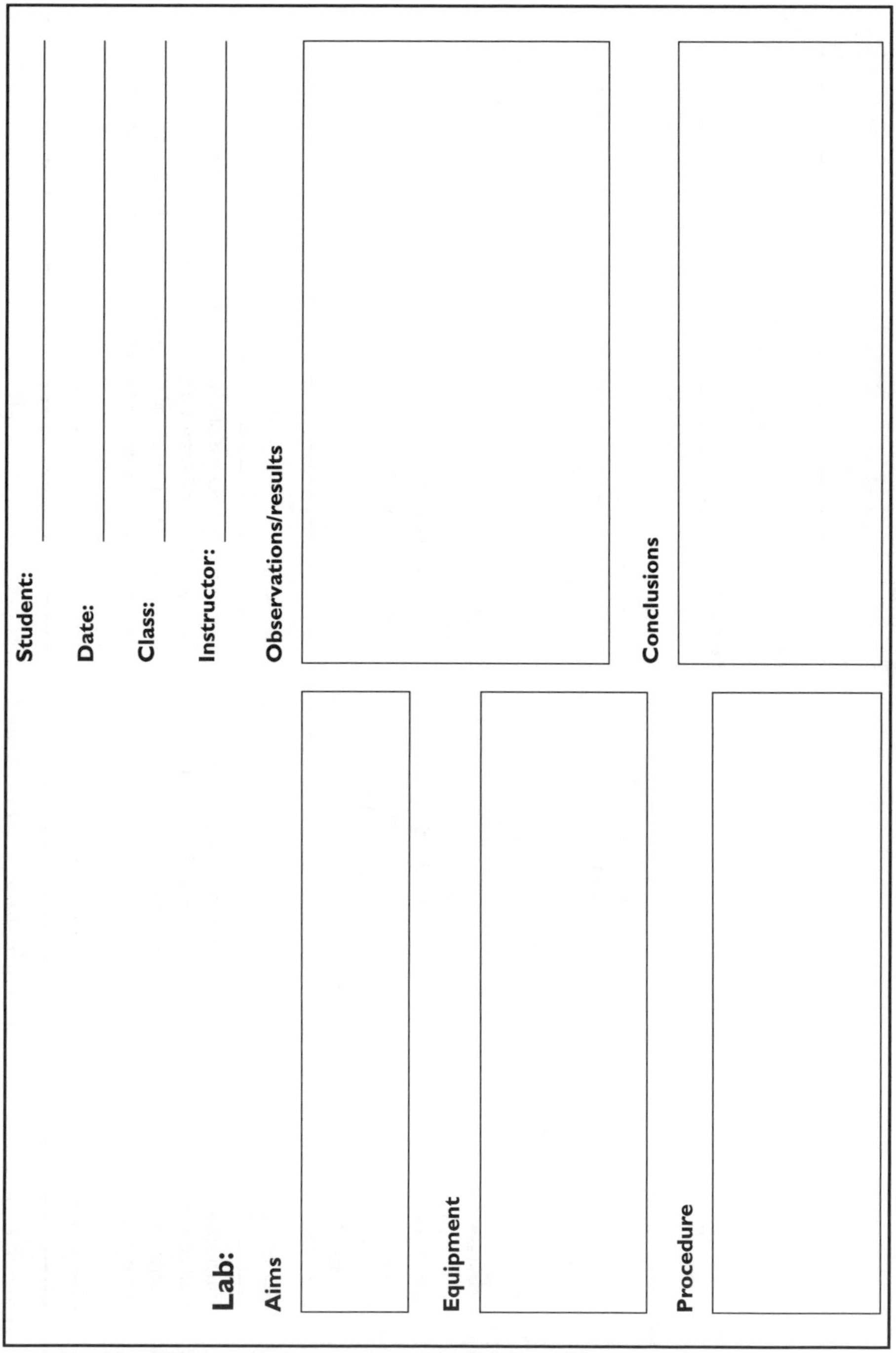

Lab:

Student:

Date:

Class:

Instructor:

Aims

Equipment

Procedure

Observations/results

Conclusions

Figure 9.3 Structure of a typical science report

Student: _____

Date: _____

Class: _____

Instructor: _____

Lab: Title of Experiment

Introduction

Include the date the experiment was performed and the date the report was submitted. State aim of experiment.

Risk Assessment

List all the chemicals used in the experiment indicating the known hazards of each and the precaution you will be taking when using the chemical. (e.g. Acid Corrosive. Avoid skin contact, wear gloves when handling.)

Procedure

The procedure should clearly and simply outline what you did so that another student reading the report and familiar with the subject would be able to understand how you did the experiment.

Results

Results should be recorded directly in the practical book at the time of measurement. Calculations can be included in this section.

Conclusions

This should relate to your AIM. Clearly and briefly state your main conclusions from your own results.

Discussion

Discuss the significance of your results; you may like to compare them to theoretical results or other results. Only do this when you are sure of the origin of the comparisons. Include any problems you had when performing the practical or in acheiving the original aims.

Figure 9.4 Sructure of a more advanced science report

The structure(s) of a report

Figures 9.3 and 9.4 show the structure of a typical scientific report, basic and more advanced.

Other typical report structures

Simple structure:

- Title page
- Contents
- Introduction
- Methodology
- Body
- Conclusion
- Recommendations
- Bibliography
- Appendices
- Glossary

Complex structure:

- Title page
- Synopsis/Abstract
- Contents page
- Introduction
- Body
- Conclusion
- Recommendations
- Bibliography
- Appendices
- Glossary.

What is a report?

Title page

This is the front sheet of the report. This should include: title, sub-title; date; author's name and position; distribution list (reader(s)' name(s)); reference number/ course details/ statements of confidentiality:

- **Title and sub-title:** usually divided by a colon. The title gives the big picture of the report – the sub-title narrows this down. Thus the sub-title gives an indication of the scope of the report – the '**terms of reference**' of the report.

- **Date:** places the report in real time.

- **Author's name and position:** when you write a college report you are often told to assume a position – public relations expert, tax consultant... You have to write the report as though you were that person. Revealing who you 'are' tells the reader where the report is 'coming from' – and thus it reveals what angle you might be expected to adopt on the topic.

- **Distribution list:** as your position as writer might be revealing with respect to the report, so might the list of readers. You would write a different report for the bank manager than for the trade union rep.

▶

Abstract

The abstract – synopsis or summary – is the essence or gist of your report. The abstract might include:

- overall aims
- specific objectives
- problem or task
- methodology or procedures
- key findings
- main conclusions
- key recommendations.

● **Tips:**
● **Journal articles typically begin with an abstract – read the journals and see how they do it.**
● **Check with your tutors to see what they expect.**
● **As the abstract refers to the whole report – write it last!**

Contents page

The contents clearly list **all** the major sections of the report, including subsections and appendices – with page numbers.

The contents page allows the reader to navigate your report. Thus use detailed, clear headings in the report – and put them all in the contents.

● **Tip:** Check out the contents pages of books. Do they help you as a reader? How? Make yours just as useful.

Introduction

The introduction should help the reader understand the what, why and how of your report. It needs:

- **Background** to the report: either why you were interested in the topic or why the report was necessary

- **Terms of reference:** the aims or scope of the investigation – its purpose or goal, any specific limitations

- **The methodology:** the research methods you used to put the report together – literature review or something more practical: interviews, questionnaires…

The body

This small word refers to the major part of your report. You do not call this section the **body**, but clearly label the different sections of the report. Each

▶

section gets its own large number, and each sub-section gets its decimal point. **Note**: When writing reports, as with essays, we have to use clear but formal English – there is no room for abbreviations or slang.

The conclusion

Each part of the body should have a conclusion. Conclusions point out the **implications** of your findings, that is, you tell your reader what they mean – tactfully.

Recommendations

Each conclusion should lead to a recommendation. Whilst the conclusions tell us what the findings mean, the recommendations tell the reader what to **do** about them (or more tactfully, suggests a range of things that might be possible).

Appendices

An appendix is something added on or attached to something. 'Appendices' is the plural of this. In this section you can show your reader some of the things that you have used to compile your report. For example, if you used interviews, you would place the interview questions there. If you circulated a questionnaire, you would place a sample questionnaire there.

Appendices do not count in the word limit for your report – but this does not mean that you can just put everything in there. Only put useful things there – and only things that you direct the reader to.

Bibliography

As with the essay:
Harvard System: Author (date) *Title*, publisher, and town of publication
British Standard System: Author, *Title*, publisher, date

Glossary

A list of unusual words. Especially useful in a report that has more than one reader: for example, a technical report that will also have to be read by a layperson (member of the public).

Presentation and style

- Neat and easy to read
- Word processed
- Consistent style: simple basic layout used consistently throughout your whole report.

● **Tip: decide where you will number, underline, embolden, italicise; save a template (pattern) – use every time you start work; check for a department style – use that!**

Why write reports?

A basic why of report writing is that reports are another form of written assessment. More importantly perhaps, there are two characteristics to reports that make them significant for you:

■ Reports on courses model the reports we will write in our jobs. Writing reports at university therefore prepares us for the work we will do.

■ Reports also model academic journal articles. Writing reports at university therefore prepares us for publishing our research – this is often another factor of the work we will do once we leave university.

Thinking about the 'why' of individual reports

However, each report that we are set to write at university is designed to investigate a particular topic – to be read by a particular reader – and to achieve a particular purpose with respect to that reader. If we focus on these things we can see some other 'whys' to report writing.

■ Why am I writing this report – what am I trying to achieve?

■ Why am I writing this report – what do I want my reader to think and do after reading my report?

Why write reports – what am I trying to achieve?

Arguably there are three main forms of reports: factual, instructional and persuasive; each has a different purpose. Think about what you are trying to achieve before you start your report.

■ **Factual:** the factual or informative report is expected to define or establish a current situation. The school report might fall into this category.

■ **Instructional:** the instructional, explanatory, report is supposed to explore a situation and suggest a range of options for further action. The *Which* report might fall into this category.

■ **Persuasive:** the persuasive or leading report is supposed to investigate a problem and suggest a specific course of action. A surveyor's report might fall into this category.

The line between these reports does become blurred at times; but do try to at least clarify your aims for yourself before you start.

Query: are you writing a report right now? Is it factual, instructional, persuasive? Will this affect you in any way?

● **Tips**
● If your report is *factual*, you will be gathering information to fully explain or define a situation.
● If your report is *instructional*, you will be gathering the information to explain a problem and offer a range of solutions.
● If your report is *persuasive*, you will be gathering the information to explain a problem and recommend just one solution.

Why write the report – what do I want my reader to think and do after reading my report?

Unlike an essay – which is often written as though for an intelligent, interested member of the public – a report is written for a specific reader or readers. These are real people.

The thing with real people is that they have wants, needs and beliefs of their own. Therefore if you want a reader to think and do what you want, you must consider the reader when planning and writing your report.

Key questions to consider here might be:

■ Who is my reader?

■ What can I expect my reader to already know about this topic?

■ How can I deal with this in my report?

■ What can I expect my reader to believe about my topic?

■ How can I deal with this in my report?

■ What can I expect my reader to want from this report?

■ How can I deal with this in my report?

■ What will I want my reader to think and do after reading my report?

■ What language, tone and style will my reader respond to?

● **Tip:** When drafting reports, think of the language, evidence and examples that will influence real readers.

How to plan and prepare a report

The preparation steps that we covered for the essay are equally valid for the report – with a few extra questions thrown in. We are going to cover them here:

Step 1: Prepare to research

■ Open a research folder – write the whole question out.

■ Analyse the question.

- Brainstorm/question matrix.
- Cross-reference with aims and outcomes.
- Think about the report dimension:
  - Why am I writing this report?
  - What is the purpose (factual/instructional/persuasive)?
  - Who is my reader?
  - What do they know?
  - What are their beliefs/attitudes?
  - What do they want from my report?
  - What will I want my reader to think?
  - What will I want my reader to do?
- Action plan – when action planning remember to follow up your 'reader' questions!

Step 2: Follow the action plan: systematic and targeted research – using the QOOQRRR system

- As always, utilise your QOOQRRR technique to target your research and get the most from your reading.
- If using interviews and questionnaires to gather information for your report – you will need to design interviews and circulate questionnaires.
- If undertaking second or third year level research, you will need to investigate the merits of quantitative research (involving large numbers of people) and qualitative research (may not involve large numbers; typically involves more in-depth interviews, the gaining of more personal responses). You will have to justify your methodology; that is, you will have to argue a case for why you have chosen a quantitative or a qualitative approach to your research.
- Make pattern notes – sourced.
- Store notes in research folder; build big topic patterns.

Step 3: Review your notes

- Remember to consider the findings from the questionnaires and/or interviews if applicable.

Step 4: Plan the body

■ Think of all the sections that the body of your report will need.

■ Think of clear titles – headings and sub-headings that you can use. Make sure that they reveal what is going on to your reader.

■ Think of the language, tone and style that will impress your potential reader.

Step 5: Write the first draft

■ As always – remember that you will draft and re-draft.

■ Keep the flow going – leave gaps and errors in your first draft.

Step 6: Leave it

■ Allow time for your brain to close the gaps.

■ Work on something else for a while.

Step 7: Review, revise and edit

■ Change what you have written.

■ Write your final draft.

■ If you have not done so before – write the introduction, conclusion and recommendations.

■ Make sure that there is a conclusion for each section of the body of your report.

■ Write a recommendation for each conclusion.

Step 8: Proof read

● **Tip:** If you look for all your mistakes at once you miss many errors. So keep a record of all the mistakes that you commonly make. Look for one of 'your' mistakes at a time. For example, perhaps you know you 'always' get your tenses wrong plus you 'always' spell certain words wrong. Go through once looking for tenses; go through again looking for spellings.

Step 9: Copy and hand in

Step 10: Getting it back

● **Tip:** When reflecting on your work, make a note of three things that you do particularly well and three things that could be improved upon. If you do this after every assessment you should be able to always identify ways of improving your performance and developing your practice.

Report checklist

■ What was my aim in writing this report? Have I achieved my goals?

■ Is the title page adequate: title and sub-title; author and position; reader and position? Date?

■ Is the title/sub-title appropriate?

■ Was an abstract necessary? Is there one? Is it clear?

■ Is there a contents page? Is it clear?

■ Is there an introduction? Does it reveal: background? Terms of reference? Methodology?

■ Are the sections and sub-sections of the body clearly labelled?

■ Does the reader get sufficient information to make the decisions I desire?

■ Is all the information necessary or have I written too much?

■ Can the reader follow the development of my ideas? Are they laid out logically?

■ Is the layout simple and consistent?

■ Are the language and tone suitable for the actual reader?

■ Is the style appropriate to the subject and reader?

■ Do I offer sufficient evidence to 'prove' my points? Do I discuss my evidence?

■ Does my conclusion follow logically from my arguments? Is there a 'conclusion' for every section of the body?

■ Have I really laid the groundwork for my recommendations? Is there a recommendation for each conclusion?

■ Should there be a glossary? Is it comprehensive?

■ Are the appendices clearly labelled? Is the reader directed to each appendix in the body of the report?

■ Is the bibliography adequate? Is it laid out in the correct way? (Remember, alphabetical order by author's surname.)

Obviously if the answer to any of these questions is No – then you must make the necessary changes!

Conclusion – the report

We have looked in some detail at the academic report – making clear links to the plan, prepare and review strategies necessary for a good academic essay. As always, we recommend that you reflect on everything that you have read here about the report – make brief, pattern notes to remind yourself of all the things that you think will help you to now plan and write a really good report on your course.

Here we call it a paper

Some university tutors refuse to speak of essays or reports. They think essays smack of school compositions and that reports are too reductionist. These tutors will speak of writing **academic papers**.

If you have a tutor like this, ask them exactly what sort of structure they require. They will probably be expecting you to lay out your writing in the journal article format. This is very much like a report – but without the numbered points.

How to prepare better presentations

Presentations are becoming an increasingly popular assessment tool – with tutors! Typically presentations were introduced onto academic programmes to acknowledge that most of us are much better at speaking than we are at writing – especially academic writing. Of course, what this strategy forgets is that students, like every normal human being on the planet, tend to be terrified of public speaking, of presentations!

We cannot make all the fear go away, but we can help you to realise that you can and will get really good at presentations if you follow the advice below. Typically, motivated students who do what is recommended here move on to get A grades for their presentations. It is as simple as that!

We are going to look at the what, why and how of presentations. With the 'how' we shall again cross-reference with our ten-step plan, prepare and review strategy – but we will also build in a specific presentation dimension, in particular we will consider the **four presentation Ps: Plan, Prepare, Practise and Present**.

Activity: Brainstorm this topic with your study partner

Take five minutes to quickly jot down what you already know about presentations, what you like and dislike about presentations and what you want to gain from this section of the book.

Compare your brainstorm with your study partner's.

Query: How do you both feel now? Typically you will realise that you are definitely not alone in your hopes and fears about presentations. You should also now be ready to move on and get the most from this section of the book.

What is a presentation?

There are several 'whats' to a presentation that we are going to cover here – they are **all** true. The trick for you, as always, is to think 'How will knowing this help me to give better presentations?'

It's just talking, isn't it?

A presentation is a formal talk of a set length usually on a set topic – to a specific, that is a knowable, audience. When preparing your presentation you have to think about these things. That is, fit the topic into the time you have been given – there is no point saying that it could not fit into five minutes! If that was the task, then that is what you have to do. You also have to pitch the topic at your actual audience. Again, as with the report, these are real people with real knowledge, thoughts and feelings. You have to make sure that your language, style and tone are just right for the real people that you are going to address. Finally you have to make sure that any audio-visual aids (AVA) – that is, supporting material like handouts, OHTs (overhead transparencies), PowerPoint, photographs, posters, etc. – will connect with your actual audience.

It's all an act

No matter what anyone else tells you, remember that a presentation is a performance. You are standing in front of people and talking to them: they are looking at and listening to you – this is a performance. Therefore you are a performer. Use this! Like any performance a presentation is an act. To make it work for you, you do not have to be happy, confident or even interested in the topic – as long as you **act** happy, confident and interested in the topic.

For if you are not happy and confident, your audience will feel uncomfortable – they will not have a good time – and it is your responsibility to make sure that they do have a good time, or that they at least learn something from you. Further, if you are not interested in the topic – why should they be? So **act** as if it is all great!

It's an act – positive body language

Remember the performance aspect of the presentation and resolve to use positive body language:

- **do** stand or sit straight

- **do not** hold anything in front of your face

- **do** smile

- **do not** tap your foot or hand or make chopping motions with your hands

▶

- **do** draw people calmly into your presentation with brief welcoming gestures

- **do not** hold your arms defensively in front of your body

- **do** stand in a relaxed manner

- **do not** stand there with clenched fists or looking as if you want to be somewhere else

- **do** dress for success

- **(in a group presentation) do not** act as if you hate everybody else on the team

- **do ACT** calm, confident and in control!

It's communication

As a performer, you will have to build a rapport with your audience – a relationship with them. You will also have to communicate and interact with them. This means that you will need to look at them – you will have to make eye contact with everybody in your audience.

So do not listen to those who say, just look at the ceiling at the back of the room. That may be okay if you have an audience of 1000 or more people, but in a small group it just looks unbalanced. You will need to look at people to draw them into your talk and take them with you. You will also need to check that they are following what you say. This will tell you whether or not to repeat or explain something – you will never discover this if you do not look at your audience.

This means that, just like an actor on the stage, you must never, ever speak from a script. You must learn your presentation and then deliver it fresh, as though for the first time. You must not read your presentation. Reading a presentation is the quickest way to lose your audience and lose any marks that were available for good communication.

The formal convention

The presentation has the same form (formal convention) as the essay – and it has the same need to address real audiences as the report. Therefore, you should have a sense of the presentation already from what you now know about essays and reports. Figure 9.5 shows the specific details of the presentation.

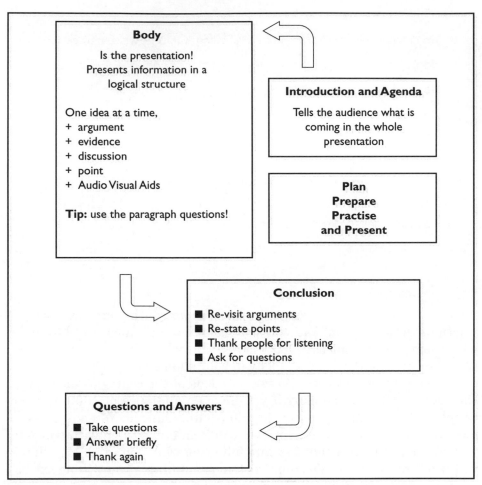

Figure 9.5 Structure of a presentation

What is a presentation?

Introduction, with a clear agenda

- introduce yourself

- give the topic title

- make opening remarks

- give the agenda of the talk.

The introduction is where you hook the audience; tell them why they should be listening to you. Are you going to be interesting, useful or funny? Will it help them pass an exam or get better grades for something? Will it save them time or effort? Think of something.

The agenda is where you tell the audience exactly what is coming in your presentation. Without an agenda the audience does not know where the talk is going. This is unsettling – and confusing. A confused audience is not a happy audience! Tell them what is coming… and this simple technique will dramatically improve the presentation itself and your marks.

The body

This is the presentation. This is where you answer the question that you were set. As with the essay, think about one big idea at a time – supported by argument and evidence – and **AVA**. Think about building a logical case.

● **Tip:** Use the paragraph questions.

The conclusion

As with the essay conclusion, this is where you draw the whole presentation together. Re-visit your main arguments, re-emphasise your main points – and use the words from the question to prove that you have answered the whole question.

● **Tips:**
● Write introductions and conclusions last.
● Introductions and conclusions can feel silly or obvious or uncomfortable – but putting them in makes an average presentation an excellent one. Just bite the bullet and do it!

The question and answer session

It's over – you want to rush out screaming! Don't! You now have to thank the audience for listening and ask them for questions.

● **Tips:**
● Do re-phrase difficult questions – check that you have understood.
● Do keep answers short.
● Do keep answers good-natured.
● Do notice when people put their hands up – take questions in order.
● Do not start fighting your audience.
● Do not try to make everyone agree with you.
● Do not think that you have to know everything (unless it is a job interview or an oral exam).
● If you cannot answer why not try: 'That is a very good question – what does everyone else think?' If no one else knows, 'Well, that has given us all something to think about. Thank you again for listening!'.
● Do bring the question and answer session to a firm end. The audience likes to know that it is all over safely.

Why do we set presentations?

As with planning and preparing any assignment, the process of preparing a presentation is designed to be an active learning process. As you plan, prepare, practise, perform and finally reflect on your presentations you are really getting to grips with and learning the material. As you think about how to communicate a topic effectively to your audience **you** are synthesizing and using information. Effectively communicating what you have learned leads you to develop a familiarity with the way your subject actually works; you become familiar with the academic practices of your subject.

It's an opportunity

And, yes, presentations really do extend the range of assessment opportunities open to you. Before you have successfully delivered and survived your first presentation you may find this hard to believe, but once you have done this, you may find that given the choice between an essay and a presentation, you would choose the presentation everytime. Once you have cracked how to do presentations well, you will realise that it is easier to get good grades for a presentation than for a piece of writing.

And a job skill

Further, good oral communication skills are definitely required by employers – some even require a formal presentation as part of the interviewing process. Developing good presentation skills over your time at university can make the difference between getting that job you want – or not.

What a gas

Finally, once you can **do** presentations, your self-esteem really improves. From the very first one that you plan, prepare, practise and present, you start to feel better about yourself as a student. This is not just something that we are telling you here to make you feel better – this is something that all our students have fed back to us – succeeding in presentations is one of the best confidence boosters they have ever had! Further, that increase in self-confidence enriches all their studies.

How to succeed in presentations

Here we will be utilising our ten-step strategy and building in a dimension specific to presentations – the four presentation Ps: plan, prepare, practise and present.

Step 1: Prepare to research

■ Open research folder.

■ Analyse the question.

■ C.f. (compare with) aims and learning outcomes.

■ Brainstorm the topic.

■ Remember it is a presentation.

P1 – Plan
Think about your time limit, your topic and your audience:
Time limit: How can you fit the topic in the time you have been allowed?
What will you have to put in – what will you have to leave out?
Topic and audience: Remember – an audience is made up of real people with real knowledge and expectations of their own. Some things to think about:

■ What can I expect my audience to know about this topic before I start?

■ What will I want them to know when I have finished (this can give you the **aims** of your presentation)?

■ How will I get them from where they are to where I want them to be (this can suggest a **logical structure** to your presentation)?

■ What language, tone and style will be right for this audience?

■ What arguments and evidence will they understand – and relate to?

■ What audio-visual aids will help – and will work with this audience?
 – think of visual aids to illustrate the topic – photographs, charts, diagrams, key quotes
 – think of visual aids that will help people follow your presentation – have the agenda on an OHT, make a large pattern note of your presentation: and display it!

■ How will my audience react to this topic? Will they be resistant, happy, frightened, interested – or not? What will I have to do to get them to respond positively?

■ What questions might they ask me? What answers will I give?

■ Action plan: now that you have considered all these things: what will you do, read, find and make to get your presentation ready?

Step 2: Targeted research – following the action plan

■ Active and interactive reading to gather information – QOOQRRR.

■ Remember to make your AVA!

Step 3: Review your findings

■ Review your notes

■ What do you now think?

■ Review your AVA – which will you use? Which don't you need?

Step 4: Plan

■ Plan the **body** of your presentation – this will give introduction/agenda and conclusion.

■ Remember – convince yourself first. If you can act as though you believe it, it will help the audience to believe you.

Step 5: Write the first draft

Remember this is a presentation – this leads us to our next presentation P.

P2 – Prepare

■ Prepare a script. If you wish to write a script – that is okay – **if you remember to destroy your script at some point**. A script draft can give you a sense that you have taken control of your presentation and organised your material to your satisfaction.

■ Prepare a set of prompts to guide you through the presentation itself. This could be:

– key words only

– key examples

– key names and dates

– notes of the key AVA. These can be written on:

cue cards – index cards with those key words upon them

a key word pattern note – numbered to guide your eye round the page

a key word list of points to make.

● **Tip:** You must not read from your script – you will be boring and dull and you will lose your audience. Recreate your presentation from the key words on your cue cards.

Step 6: Leave it!

Allow the brain to close the gaps that you have left in your presentation.

Step 7: Review, revise and edit

We have adapted this to fit getting a presentation ready – so this also becomes a presentation P.

P3 – Practise

Once you have a shape to your presentation, with your prompts prepared to help you recreate your presentation, you are now ready to practise – to rehearse.

Rehearsal is vital to a successful presentation

You must not say the presentation for the first time in front of an audience – it will not be 'polished' and the words will sound extremely strange to you. This is not a good thing. You must be comfortable with your presentation.

There are two key stages to your rehearsal:

1 Refine and polish (review, revise and edit)

Your first rehearsals allow you to review, revise and edit your presentation – to refine and finish it. This is very similar to going over your essay so that all the gaps are closed, the boring bits are tidied up and the overlong sentences are shortened so that they become clear and effective.

● **Tip:** Use the paragraph questions to shape the parts of your presentation.

It will help to refine your presentation if you rehearse in front of a *critical friend* who will give you useful feedback.

● **Tip:** Do not rehearse in front of your children. Our mature students always feed back that their children tend to say 'it's boring, it's silly'… leaving them feeling really discouraged.

A critical friend can tell you what is good about your presentation. They can tell you what is working, what is easy to follow and understand. But they can also tell you what is not working. Where they do not follow you or your meaning is unclear.

● **Tip: Listen to this feedback!** Do not just shout at the critical friend and tell them that they do not understand. If they cannot understand, it means that you are not yet communicating effectively. Change your presentation until they can understand – quickly and easily.

2 Learn the presentation

Once your presentation is as good as it can be, you need to rehearse to learn it. Here you need to practise with your cue cards and your AVA. You need to do this until you know your presentation really well – until you could do it in your sleep.

Then you need to practise some more until you can say it every time as though you are saying it for the first time! This will keep your presentation fresh and hence it will appeal to and grip your audience.

Step 8: 'Proof read' (check your own presentation skills)

For really important presentations – assessed ones that carry a high percentage of your course marks, oral exams and job interviews – as well as using a critical friend, consider videotaping your rehearsals and checking yourself. In both cases – use the checklist.

Presentation checklist

For use by your critical friend – or you if you are reviewing yourself on video.

■ Check the introduction. Does it tell the audience what you are talking about and why? Does it have a 'hook' telling the audience why they should listen to you? Does it give a clear agenda telling people the 'order' of your talk?

■ Do you have a logical structure?

■ Does each part of the presentation answer the paragraph questions? Do you discuss your evidence? Do you make points?

■ Do you signpost clearly? That is, do you tell people what is happening and where you are going? (Also known as using the linguistic or discourse markers, put more simply this means – do you clearly indicate your progress through the presentation: we have looked at this – now we are moving on to…?)

■ Do you have a conclusion that revisits your main arguments and re-states your main points?

■ Do you have any strange tics, mannerisms or gestures that you might like to get rid of (do not fiddle with a pen or scratch your nose!).

■ Will your AVA support your talk or distract from it? Will everybody be able to see at once?

● **Tips:**
● Think about writing up your agenda – and speaking it.
● Never pass anything around because that really disrupts a presentation.
● Make handouts simple and clear – if they are too detailed people will start reading and they will not listen.
● Put only a few words on OHTs or flip charts – make them big enough for everybody to see. Again, too many words and they will read and not listen.
● Let people see what you are showing them before you take visual aids away.

▶

● Remove visuals when you are finished with them so that they do not distract the audience from your next point.
● If you want people to see then make notes, you will have to stop speaking long enough for them to do so.

Examine your practice presentation and improve it.

Step 9: Hand it in

Ah, but we cannot hand in a presentation and go away while it gets marked in our absence! We have to deliver or perform a presentation. So this takes us to our fourth presentation P.

P4 – Present

To make sure that your presentation proper is as good as it can be – we have boxed some tips and tricks of things to do before and during your presentation.

Presentation day – tips and tricks

Okay – you are going to be nervous. Do not focus on that – think positive and get on with it. Here are some things to do:

Before

1   Work on being positive!

● **Tips:** Read Chapter 7 How to build your confidence. Practise your positive thinking. Keep saying: 'I am prepared.' 'This is a great presentation.'

2   On your way to your presentation, run through your main points – with and without your cue cards. Reassure yourself that you do know it.

3   Get to the room early so you will be as cool, calm and collected as you can be. Rushing in late will increase your stress levels.

4   Organise the seating – take control of the environment. Where will you want people to sit so that you feel good and they can all hear you? Do you want them in rows, in a semi-circle, sitting on the floor?

● **Tip:** Arrange to stand behind a desk or a lectern. This small barrier between you and your audience will help you feel safe and in control.

▶

5 Check that the equipment is working.

● **Tip:** Have a back up system in place – if using OHTs, have some photocopies of your OHT pages to circulate as handouts if the OHP (over-head projector) does not work.

6 Use your adrenalin – it will help you think on your feet.

7 Be positive again: Say, 'I am prepared.' And, 'I can handle this.'

8 If too stressed (before or during a presentation):

- Stop.

- Sigh.

- Drop your shoulders. (We hold our shoulders up when tense and this increases tension.)

- Wriggle your toes. (We clench our feet when stressed and this increases our blood pressure and hence our stress levels.)

- Unclench your fists – this is a typical anger/fear reaction – let it go!

- Take a few deep, slow breaths. Deep quick ones and you **will** pass out!

- Start again more slowly.

9 Write your agenda on the board, on a handout, on an OHT or on the flip chart.

During

Remember to:

1 Introduce yourself and your topic.

2 Give a brief introduction and **say** your agenda even if it is written up.

3 Speak slowly and clearly. Let people hear and follow you.

4 If you get lost – don't panic! Pause, look at your prompts, carry on.

5 Remember the linguistic markers – we have … now we are…

6 Make good eye contact – look at everyone in the room.

● **Tip: Do** stand so that you can see everyone and everyone can see you. **Don't** stare madly at one person so that they want to get up and leave!

7 Use your AVA with confidence. Make sure everyone can see everything. Allow people to notice what is there before you take it away.

8 Remember your conclusion – re-visit and re-state… no matter how silly it seems. Your audience does not know the topic as well as you do – they will need to be reminded of what you have talked about and what it means.

9 Thank people for listening – ask for questions.

10 Chair the Q&A session fairly – keep those answers short and sweet. Bring the Q&A to a firm conclusion. Thank people again.

Step 10: Reviewing your presentation

As with the essay and the report, it is useful for you to be able to review and evaluate your own presentations. However, because of the especially emotional dimension of presentations, we recommend that you undertake this in two stages:

1 Immediately after your presentation, tell yourself what a wonderful presentation it was and how brave you were for giving it. Try not to dwell on everything that went wrong – for that just makes it feel harder to do a presentation next time. So make this first review a very positive one.

2 As with your writing, after some time has elapsed, it becomes useful for you to undertake a more detailed SWOT analysis of your presentation:

■ What were your strengths? What did you do very well? What sections of the presentation were you particularly pleased with? Why? Make notes so that you remember. Sometimes we are so busy correcting our faults that we forget to repeat our strengths.

■ What were your weaknesses? What did not go so well? Why was this? Was it *form* – perhaps it was not structured or presented properly? Was it *content* – was it a poor argument unsupported by evidence? Did you forget to discuss your evidence? Did you forget to refer back to the question?

■ Opportunities: Now, go on, try to think of just how good you can become at presentations and of all the opportunities this gives you, both as a student and in future employment.

■ Threats: If you are still feeling threatened by presentations, what are you going to do next? Will you practise more? Do you need more support with your positive thinking? Do you need to find a study partner? Do you need to seek out Learning Development or Support and get some more help?

For all these things – don't forget to make notes of what you will need to do – and when you will do these things.

● **Tips:**
● Don't forget to use your tutor feedback.
● Don't forget to use video play back to refine your performance.

Conclusion – the presentation

We have now looked in some detail at the academic presentation, paying particular attention to 'what' – that they are talks of set length, on set topics, to set audiences. Here we stressed how particular audiences have to be predicted and catered for. We looked at why we set – and you do – presentations. As always we considered the heuristic (active learning) dimension of presentations. We also emphasised that developing good presentation skills will prepare you for employment and increase your self-confidence whilst encouraging you to access an assessment mode in which you should be able to shine relatively quickly. With 'how' we returned to the ten-step programme that we have already covered in the essay and the report – but here we added the four Ps of the presentation: plan, prepare, practise and present, to emphasise the specific aspects of oral rather than written assignments. **(That was a conclusion – see how it re-visits the main arguments and then highlights the main points? It is as simple as that.)**

As always, please make your own key word pattern notes of the points that you wish to remember – and use. None of this will make a difference unless and until you put it into practice!

Presentation activities

Some things to think about and do to improve your presentation skills.

I   **The three-minute presentation**: Before giving a presentation for your course work, prepare and deliver a three minute presentation to your study partner or study group. Choose a simple topic like a hobby or a holiday, just to get you started.

With this presentation just get the *form* right – introduction, agenda; body (logical structure – AVA); conclusion; Q&A. This will build your confidence for your assignment.

● **Tip:** Use the presentation checklist to evaluate yourself – ask your friend to complete one for you, too.

▶

2 Practise with a critical friend. Before an assignment presentation, practise in front of your study partner. Use their feedback.

3 Team work. If asked to prepare and deliver a group presentation, remember to **practise with your group**.

● **Tips: Do** look like a group – this could mean dressing in similar colours. **Do** act as though you were a good group that worked really well together (even if you hate each other!).

How to prepare better seminars

The academic seminar is typically used as a formative assessment tool designed to help students develop an important academic paper. Therefore seminars are often part of research degrees, especially of PhDs; however, they can form part of any programme of study.

If you are asked to prepare a seminar on a topic about which you are also writing, try to get the most from the opportunity. Typically it will mean that at some point in your research, you will be expected to offer the ideas that you have formed to your peers for discussion. Usually you will be expected to write an academic paper, deliver a presentation and lead a discussion amongst a group of your peers. You will then use the discussion to seed further research of your own.

If you are set a seminar on your programme of study, embrace it. You will be fully prepared for it if you both refer back to our sections on the essay, report and presentation – and utilise the tips below. If you get a good discussion going in a seminar of your own, you will end up with a really improved final paper. Here we are going to look briefly at the what, why and how of the academic seminar.

What is a seminar?

Typically a seminar is made up of four parts:

1 Paper – prepared by you (seminar leader)

● **Tip:** Check with the tutor as to what form the paper should take – essay, report, journal article.

2 Presentation – given by you on the seminar topic, but not just the paper read aloud.

3 Discussion – not just a question and answer session. That is, you must make sure that the audience engages with your ideas in some

way. Typically you should set discussion topics for the audience – and then you will have to make sure that the audience actually does engage in a discussion.

4 Summative conclusion – that is you, the seminar leader, have to draw together everything that was covered in the paper, in the presentation and in the group discussion. You should also be aware of how this will all help to shape the next step of your research.

Why engage in seminars?

As we have indicated in the opening remarks above, the seminar is a highly developed university activity. It is designed to feed student research into a collaborative learning process.

If you are giving a seminar you will have to organise your thinking in order to present your ideas in both written and oral form. This will develop your critical faculties. You will have to consider which areas of your research will benefit from group discussion; this will develop your team work and leadership skills as you organise and then manage that discussion.

For those attending a seminar, it is a chance to participate in their colleagues' research; it can be an interesting and intense active and interactive learning experience. It can model good practice for participants as they get to read other students' papers – and hear other students' presentations. This is a very good thing. Finally, as this is a high-level university activity, engaging in seminars allows and enables you to refine your academic practice.

How to plan, prepare and benefit from seminars

As this draws on the work already covered in this chapter, this is offered just as a key point summary – with annotations that highlight specific seminar points.

The 10-step seminar programme

1 Prepare to research:

- analyse the question/topic

- check course aims and learning outcomes

- brainstorm, use a question matrix

- action plan – think of paper, presentation, discussion topics.

2 Targeted research using QOOQRRR.

3 Review notes.

4 Plan the whole seminar:

- plan paper
- plan presentation
- plan discussion topics – and discussion strategy.

● **Tip: Do** set questions that will help your own research. **Do** divide the audience into small groups and give each group a question (different or the same). Allow a set time for discussion. Hold a plenary to get feedback from the groups.

- plan overall conclusion.

● **Tip:** You will know what is to be in your paper and presentation, you can prepare concluding remarks for those. Then you must be prepared to make notes on the feedback that you get from your discussion groups, add those to your overall conclusion.

5 Prepare first drafts – of paper, presentation and of discussion topics.

6 Leave a gap.

7 Review, revise and edit.

8 Proof read: rehearse:

- the presentation
- managing a discussion
- giving a summative conclusion.

9 Deliver with confidence:

- paper, in advance
- presentation, with AVA
- discussion: questions; organised interaction
- summative conclusion. **Note**: the easiest marks to get, and the easiest to throw away, are those awarded for the final, overall, conclusion. Do not leave this out!

10 Review own strengths and weaknesses:

- the presentation
- managing a discussion
- giving a summative conclusion
- **and then** – in the light of the discussion that you managed, and the summative conclusion that you gave, you would then have to decide what to do and read to improve your research and write a better final paper.

The advantages and disadvantages of seminars

As with any group or collaborative learning experience there are advantages and disadvantages to the seminar.

Advantages:

- collaborative learning

- active and interactive learning

- intense learning experience

- extends knowledge of a topic

- models good practice – paper, presentation, discussion techniques

- develops research angles

- improves grades in associated dissertation and essay work

- develops personal, interpersonal and communication skills

- develops organisation and time management skills.

Disadvantages:

- lack of commitment in the seminar leader produces an uncomfortable event

- poor techniques – e.g. reading a paper instead of giving a presentation – switches audiences off

- ill-prepared discussions become embarrassing

- ill-managed discussions can become exclusive, alienating or confrontational

- lack of commitment in an audience can mean that little or no learning actually takes place.

Obviously all the disadvantages can be turned into advantages with the proper planning and commitment.

Conclusion – the seminar

The academic seminar draws together oral and written communication skills. In the 'what' of the seminar we emphasised the importance of utilising what you already know about preparing essays, reports and pre-sentations. We also really stressed the importance of organising and managing a good discussion that will both interest your audience and seed your own research. In 'why' we stressed that the seminar is an active, interactive learning event that will benefit both seminar giver and the other seminar participants – if they are all committed to the venture. In 'how' we revisited the ten-step plan, prepare and review strategy, paying particular attention to the importance of the discussion and the summative conclusion. Further we emphasised how reviewing the seminar should seed your research so that your final paper is significantly better than it would have been without the seminar itself.

As always, please make your key word pattern notes – what do you want to take away about the seminar? What will you do with the information? When will you do it?

Review points

When reviewing your notes on this chapter – how to prepare better assignments, you might realise that:

- You can now look at assessment in a more positive light.

- You are prepared to engage in 'writing to learn' as opposed to writing up what you know.

- You are ready for the 'struggle to write' – it does not mean that there is anything wrong with you.

- You now think of communicating successfully in your assignments – in essays you will consider the paragraph questions, in reports you will think of reaching real readers and in presentations you will consider the audience.

- You now feel ready to tackle the essay, report, presentation and seminar.

- You realise the importance of the 10-step plan, prepare and review strategy.

- You have made links with the other sections of the book, especially managing your time, utilising the overview, being creative with a question, making pattern notes and engaging in targeted research and active reading.

10 How to be reflective – review, review, review!

Aims

It is the intention of this chapter to revisit revision practices – we will also link revision and review strategies with personal study and self-assessment, with a special focus on reviewing your development in terms of the study and academic skills and practices covered in this book.

Learning outcomes

By the end of reading this chapter and engaging in the activities set you will:

- understand the importance of the reflective review as an essential part of the learning process

- have engaged in specific review activities designed to get you reflecting on your development of the study and academic skills and practices necessary for becoming a successful student

- have re-emphasised the 'six steps to success' covered in *Essential Study Skills*

- utilised the opportunity to practise several review activities.

Introduction

Welcome to the last chapter of this text. We would just like to remind you that although this chapter comes at the end of the book, it is not the least important chapter. As we mentioned in the introduction, a book has a linear – a to b to c – format. This means that something has to come first, second and third – but in terms of successful academic practice, review is just as important as everything else that we have covered here. Further, review is something that you should be engaged in all the time, for without review there is no learning.

In this section we are going to suggest a significant review strategy – the reflective learning diary; we will move on to offer some self-assessment pointers – and activities – with respect to your evaluation of your development of the various study and academic skills and practices offered within this book. We shall draw all this together by revisiting the six steps to success that we mentioned in the Introduction – and that have shaped the information and advice in this book.

Reflective learning

When looking at pattern notes (Chapter 6) we encouraged you to engage in a revision cycle after every notemaking session – lecture, reading, discussion. We stressed that Buzan's research on the memory indicated that without active revision 98% of what has been covered would be forgotten in just three weeks. This emphasis on instant and ongoing revision also informs our advice on an overall revision strategy – SQP4 (Chapter 5). That is, revision is something that should start at the beginning of a course – and it should go on all the way through. We pointed out that this is different from *ad hoc* revision strategies where at best students might try to learn material covered in a whole programme of study in the few weeks immediately preceding an exam.

It would be wonderful if by this stage of your reading of this book you were be in a position to say, 'I have tried that and it does work!' However, we have found that students usually need more encouragement than that to take up review and revision strategies. That is why we are returning to the topic now. In this section we are going to explore the reflective learning diary, suggesting an active revision strategy that you can put into operation immediately. If you do this you will find that you are actively learning your course material.

What is a reflective learning diary?

Put very simply, the reflective learning diary (or log or journal) is an analytical and detailed, but concise, record of your studies. Typically we recommend that you spend a few minutes after each study period – a class, lecture or independent study – completing your journal. You have hopefully noticed by now that we do include review prompts and review points throughout this text in order to get you into the habit of ongoing, active review, so you have been prepared for the process of active reflection already.

When you first start engaging in the more structured reflective activity of the diary, it will most probably take you some time. You will be unfamiliar with it – and this does cost time. As with everything else that we recommend, this does get easier and quicker with practice. So do practise – and do give yourself the time to become familiar with and confident in doing your reflective learning diaries. When completing these learning diaries we advise that you complete them using the headings below.

● **Tips:**
● Keep a diary for each module that you do.
● See Fig 10.1 – Learning Diary example

The reflective learning diary

The diary structure that we recommend has five parts: what, why, reaction, learned and goal setting. This does not have to be a rigid thing – experiment until you find a structure that best meets your needs and suits your learning style.

● **Tip:** Write your diaries on one side of a piece of paper and use a pattern note format for your reviews. Use key words to make them manageable and colour and cartoons to make them memorable.

■ **What:** Make brief notes of what you did. Here you can record the lecture or seminar that you attended or the reading that you have done.

■ **Why:** Make brief analytical notes – why was this activity useful? What learning outcomes did it cover? What part of the assignment question is it helping you with? Knowing why you are doing something helps you move from passive to active learner.

■ **Reaction:** Make brief notes on your emotional response to the activity in which you engaged or the information that you received. This part of the review allows you to notice the affective dimension to your learning. It allows you to build a picture of yourself as a learner and as a student.

Here you should begin to notice the subjects and topics that you enjoy. It will also start to tell you the activities that you prefer – that is, whether you like lectures or reading, whether you enjoy group work or independent study. This allows you to choose modules and teaching and learning strategies that suit your subject interests and your learning style preferences.

● **Tips:**
● Be honest. You will not get a true picture of your own likes, dislikes and preferences if you paint a rosy picture of yourself.
● Use the discoveries that you make here to inform your subject choices.
● Use the information to help you refine your own learning style.

■ **Learned:** Make brief notes on all that you think that you learned from the lecture, class or reading. These notes are where you make your learning conscious. Making our learning conscious in this way improves both the quantity and quality of our learning. When we do not do this we are in danger of leaving the learning behind as we walk away from that lecture or close that book! You can make this section of your review as detailed or concise as you wish.

● **Tips:**
● When making the learning conscious, make links with the assignment question.
● Use this section of your review to practise your academic writing.
● Diaries, as with all academic writing, get easier with practice.

■ **Goal setting:** Make brief notes about what you could now do following the information you gained from the lecture, class or reading. Remember, we continually stress that no one lecture or piece of reading will ever give you 'all you need to know' on a subject. Therefore, when you have engaged in one activity, you should note what you need to do next.

● **Tip:** When noting what you will do next, note **when** you will do it. If you do not make a date to do it, it will not get done.

> 'Without doing my review, I wouldn't even have understood the class, let alone remembered it!'

Conclusion

We have prompted you to reinforce your active learning by using the reflective learning diary – an ongoing and detailed review system that will allow you to make your learning conscious. This will improve both the quantity and quality of your learning. This particular review structure will also enable you to notice the subjects and learning strategies that suit you best. This is information that can inform your module choices – and your learning strategies – and thus your development as a successful student.

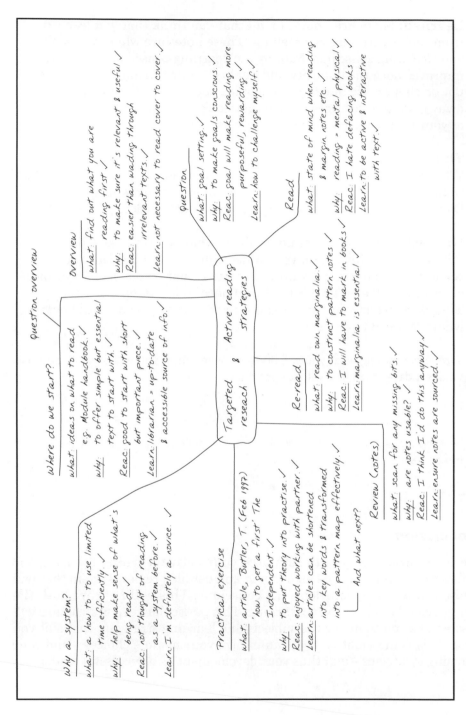

Figure 10.1 Example of a pattern review completed by student

Review points – self-assessment

As well as engaging in ongoing review – in your learning diary, with your revision cycle and in your revision folders – from time to time you should pause and reflect on your overall development as a student, as a learner. These reflective moments can focus on any aspect of your development that you wish – from how you organise your time to how well you feel you are mastering the epistemology (theory of knowledge) of your subject.

To start this reflective process off for you, in this section we are going to prompt you to reflect on the various study and academic skills and practices that we have introduced in this book.

We have interspersed our overall reflection questions with some specific activities to help you review your progress in a particular area – for example, there is a combined active reading and pattern notemaking activity, an examination skills activity, and a writing review activity.

Self-assessment – What have you done with Essential Study Skills?

We have included a brief reminder of – and reflective questions on – every section of this book. Please work through the questionnaire, answering the questions and completing the additional activities as you go.

At the end of this review you should have a picture of yourself as a student, at this moment in time. You can then decide to work on specific study or academic skills of your own that you think could do with development.

The questionnaire

1 How to learn and study

- Learning and studying

- University people and places

- The nature of your subject – what counts as knowledge? What counts as argument and evidence?

- Review your notes of this section. What are your notes like?

- What have you done with the information?

- How has reading about these things helped you so far? Think of an example.

- What will you do next?

2 How to organise yourself for study

■ Organisation and time management – when, where and how to study

– Review your notes of this section. What are your notes like?

– What have you done with the information?

– How has reading about these things helped you so far? Think of an example.

– What will you do next?

3 How to research and read academically

■ Targeted research and active reading – QOOQRRR

– Review your notes of this section. What are your notes like?

– What have you done with the information?

– How has reading about these things helped you so far? Think of an example.

– What will you do next?

Activity: Review your QOOQRRR and your pattern notemaking

Task: Read the e-mail below and make pattern notes. Note: this e-mail is a piece of academic writing that is not as formal as either a journal article or an essay.

■ **Question** – Why would an activity like this be in the book? What do you hope to gain from it? Re-read your learning contract for the book.

■ **Overview** – How does this activity fit into the book as a whole? Remind yourself of the aims and outcomes for the book.

■ **Overview** – Read the beginning and end of the e-mail – scan the first sentences. Decide what the e-mail is about.

■ **Question** – What is interesting about the e-mail? Ask yourself: Why should I read it? What can I get out of it?

■ **Read** – Once you know why you are reading the e-mail, choose which sections to read in depth. Read these through actively and interactively, marking up the text. Underline key words and points. Make margin notes. Make notes of any links – e.g. between points in the e-mail and sections of this book.

▶

■ **Re-read** – Re-read your own marginalia. Construct your own key word pattern notes. Put the key word for the central topic in the centre of an A4 sheet of paper. Draw out branches and make connections from the central topic – put in subsidiary words. Use colour and highlighters. Draw pictures to illustrate key points.

■ **Review your notes.** Are they useable? Are they sourced? Plug any gaps.

E-mail on academic practices versus study skills (26 Feb 2002)

What I am suggesting is that the identity-practice model of learning and skill, which I have been working on for some years both for the PhD and for various conference papers and articles, provides a significant move on from the 'skills-as-possessions' (like tools) model. The emphasis should be, I would argue, on getting students to become familiar with, and practised or rehearsed in, those practices which are associated with (a) being an undergraduate and then (b) being a graduate. This is, of course, congenial with the Situated Learning Theory Approach of Lave and Wenger ('legitimate peripheral participation'), but I have taken the identity issue further in terms of what I dub the 'claim-affirmation model of emergent identity'.

Particular forms of writing (and reading and talking) may be seen as examples of the practices associated with the identity of an undergraduate, and also of a graduate. Academic writing encompasses a range of types, particularly papers written for an academic audience – for a conference (or seminar, symposium, colloquium etc), for an academic journal, book etc. The purpose is (or should be) to present an argument in support of a knowledge-claim. The criteria for judging such an argument would include its location wrt [with respect to] existing, broadly accepted (and also contested) knowledge-claims (the existing literature), the logical reasoning and the empirical evidence adduced. The style should be that which is generally accepted, including conventions for citations etc.

So by the time they graduate, the students should be familiar with such a style through examination of e.g. journal articles – not focussing on the content as something-to-be-learnt but on how the author attempts to present their knowledge-claim. To write such a paper would require the student to read with a purpose (contribution to the argument to be presented), to summarise key points from the materials read for the purpose of advancing the claim, to construct a cogent article, to keep a note of bibliographic details in order to cite as appropriate, and so on. Above all, it requires the student to have something to say that is worth saying, their own voice wrt the issues at hand.

But to get there, as educators we need to help students to become adept at the various elements – peripheral participation in the practices of the community of academic practice, as Lave and Wenger might put it.

▶

There are other modes of writing that graduates should be able to undertake, orientated towards arenas of professional practice outside academia – reports, briefing papers, etc. These too can be considered in terms of the various practices that constitute the elements for producing such forms of writing. But we need to ensure students recognise that these are different, and are appropriate for different contexts and arenas of practice.

I don't think that this is particularly revolutionary – but I would emphasise the notion of practices associated with relevant identities. In mundane discourse we might talk of 'skills', but we must see them as ways of acting, not possessions which cause, or are used in, forms of action. 'Skills development' work still has an important place – more so, as it provides the basis for enabling students to practise and rehearse, and continue to do so, rather than being seen as remedial and something which is at some point finished – been there, done that, got the T-shirt.

Hope this makes sense. If you can stand reading some of my writing on this, the relational skills and learning website is at www.re-skill.org.uk. Obviously the later stuff is more fully developed.

Regards,

Len

When you have finished this activity – review your progress with your study partner:

▪ What was your first response to the e-mail? Did you get angry, frustrated, confused or happy? Remember, there are no correct reactions – but do note how you are reacting to academic language and argument at the moment.

▪ What has this activity told you about your QOOQRRR skills?

▪ What has it told you about your pattern notemaking skills?

▪ What has it told you about academic practices?

▪ What will you do now:

  – About your research and reading skills?

  – About your notemaking skills?

  – About your familiarity with academic practices?

▪ When will you do these things?

Now look at Fig 10.2 – a pattern note of the email

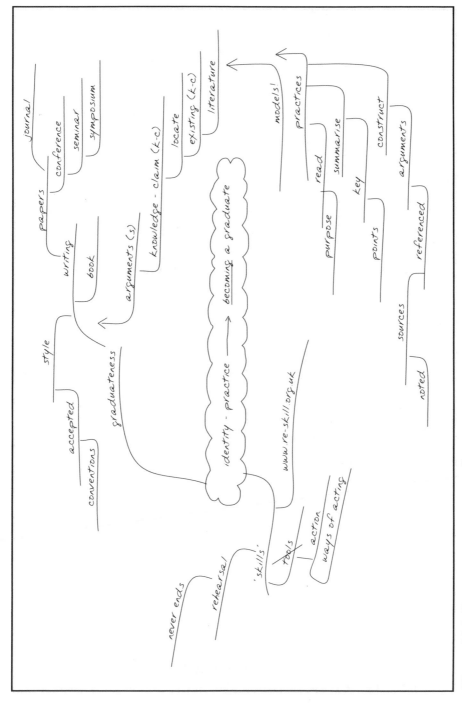

Figure 10.2 Pattern note on an e-mail

4 How to use the overview

■ Use of the overview – get the big picture – aims and learning outcomes

– Review your notes of this section. What are your notes like?

– What have you done with the information?

– How has reading about these things helped you so far? Think of an example.

– What will you do next?

5 How to succeed in exams

■ Big picture – small steps – memory and learning style; SQP4: active revision – folders – pruning notes – practise brainstorming and timed writing

– Review your notes of this section. What are your notes like?

– What have you done with the information?

– How has reading about these things helped you so far? Think of an example.

– What will you do next?

Activity: Revising exam technique

The study skills exam

Just for fun, we have included a possible exam paper for students of this book. If you want to see how well you would do under timed conditions, why not have a go at this exam. Afterwards you can reflect on how well you did – and what that tells you about yourself as a student.

Study Skills Exam

Instructor: Name:
                   Class:
                   Period:
                   Date:

Candidates must answer two questions: ONE question from Section A and ONE question from Section B. You have 90 minutes for the whole paper.

▶

Section A

I   Evaluate the usefulness of a Study Skills book to you as a student.

2   Consider the value of building on your own learning style.

3   What aspects of Study Skills will you take with you either into further study or into your work? Give reasons for your answer.

Section B

4   Consider the value of planning, preparing and writing an academic essay.

5   In what ways have you been able to use your whole study programme as a Study Skills laboratory? With this in mind, what advice would you give next year's students?

6   Evaluate the usefulness to you as a student of one of the following: active learning; trial and error; self-assessment. Give examples to justify your answer.

Exam ends

Query: How well did you do? If you are not sure, ask your study partner to mark your answers and to give you feedback. But here are some things for you to think about:

■ Did you follow instructions? Did you answer one question from each section? If not, you know that you will need to keep practising this!

■ Did you brainstorm/plan before you wrote your answer? Did this help? Do you need more practice at brainstorming? When will you do this? If you did not brainstorm – why not? If in doubt – go to Chapter 6 on creative learning. Remember that brainstorming, like everything else we do, does indeed get better with practice.

● **Tip:** Why not brainstorm every question on this paper just to practise brainstorming? Do this with your study partner – allow yourselves ten minutes per question, then compare brainstorms at the end.

■ Did you manage your time well? What have you learned about your ability to manage time? What do you need to practise to get better at managing your time?

■ Overall: what have you learned about yourself as an exam taker? Make sure you do something with this information.

6 How to learn creatively

■ Creativity is vital

■ Pattern notes

■ Brainstorming and question matrixing assignment questions

- Review your notes of this section. What are your notes like?
- What have you done with the information?
- How has reading about these things helped you so far? Think of an example.
- What will you do next?

7 How to build your confidence

■ Effect and affect; the role of feelings

■ Feelings about being a student

■ Positive thinking

- Review your notes of this section. What are your notes like?
- What have you done with the information?
- How has reading about these things helped you so far? Think of an example.
- What will you do next?

8 How to succeed in group work

■ Academic groups, forms and processes, building for your c.v.

- Review your notes of this section. What are your notes like?
- What have you done with the information?
- How has reading about these things helped you so far? Think of an example.
- What will you do next?

9. How to prepare better assignments

■ Assessment

■ Communication

■ Understanding of essay, report, presentation and seminar as conventions and academic practices – structures – argument – evidence – paragraph questions – communicating

- Review your notes of this section. What are your notes like?
- What have you done with the information?

   – How has reading about these things helped you so far? Think of
     an example.

   – What will you do next?

Activity: Overcoming writing blocks

This is an activity you can try on your own – or with other people around you.
Each person will need two pieces of paper plus pens and pencils.

1   Find a space in which you think that you would be able to write.

2   Settle down with two pieces of paper in front of you – and all the pens and
pencils that you could want. Label one piece of paper – writing. Label the
other piece of paper – commentary.

3   Give yourself a set time to write – at least 15 minutes and up to 30 minutes.

4   Settle down to write about anything that you can hear, see, feel or smell at
the time of writing. Write continuously. Do not stop.

● **Tip: Do not worry about this or debate it – just start writing. Do not
put the exercise off – do it!**

5   Every time you do stop writing, put the reason for stopping on the
commentary sheet of paper. No matter what the reason is – how silly, or
small or trivial – make a note of it.

6   After your set writing time, stop writing.

7   Review all the different reasons you gave for stopping. Notice what your
reasons for stopping are.

8   If you have been working with other people, discuss all the different reasons
given for stopping writing.

9   Work out what to 'do' about some of your different reasons for stopping.

Reasons that other students have given:

■ Stopping to search for the right word

■ Checking my spelling

■ Wondering whether I've got the sentence right

■ Checking my grammar and tenses

■ I kept checking the time

■ Thinking of a new idea

▶

■ I was trying to think of a better idea

■ It was too hot

■ I felt too cold

■ I was uncomfortable, I kept wriggling in my chair

■ I was thirsty

■ I was hungry

■ I heard a noise

■ Someone left the room and I wondered what they were doing

Query: do you notice anything about these points? Are they anything like your reasons for stopping?

Discussion:

There appear to be certain 'sets' of reasons for stopping work:

■ Searching for words and spellings, checking that the work is correct.

■ Thinking of new ideas.

■ Feeling uncomfortable. Being hungry or thirsty or too hot or cold. Checking the time. Not feeling right in the chair. Wondering what people are doing.

Query:

Is there anything we can 'do' about these things? Think about it first – then move on to our suggestions.

1 Thinking of words and spellings and generally getting it 'right'.

We have tackled this in Chapter 9 – how to prepare better assignments. Remember, here we talked about accepting that you will draft and re-draft your work. Therefore in first drafts try not to go for perfection. Put in the wrong word, do not worry about getting all the spellings and tenses right. When stuck for a word put in an ellipsis (dot dot dot) and move on. The trick with getting a first draft down is to keep the 'flow' going. Definitely do not interrupt your flow of ideas for in doing that you will lose the thread of your thinking.

● **Tip: Practise using the ellipsis to keep your flow going. Accept the notion of drafting and re-drafting work.**

2 Searching for ideas.

Again we tackled this in Chapter 9. Plan your writing before you write. At least brainstorm a few key ideas to get a rough shape to your work. Write once you have a plan, then follow your plan.

▶

● **Tip:** Practise brainstorming and planning.

3 General feelings of discomfort.
This could mean that you have not yet sorted out your 'where to write'. Perhaps you need to do a bit more work on your organisation – plan when, where and how you will study. To help you do this, consider your individual learning style. Remember there is no one correct way of working. Some people like quiet, some like noise. Some like bright lights, some definitely do not. Some people like to sit still, some like to move around. What sort of learning style suits you?

● **Tip:** Practise your see, hear, do and say strategies. Read around the topic of learning style.

After reflecting on these topics – plan what you need to do next, and when you need to do it!

10 How to be reflective

- Remembering revision – the revision cycle and SQP4 (Chapter 5)

- Reflective learning diaries

- Review yourself – self-assessment

  – Review your notes of this section. What are your notes like?

  – What have you done with the information?

  – How has reading about these things helped you so far? Think of an example.

  – What will you do next?

● **Tip:** See Figure 10.3, student self-assesment following a study skills programme.

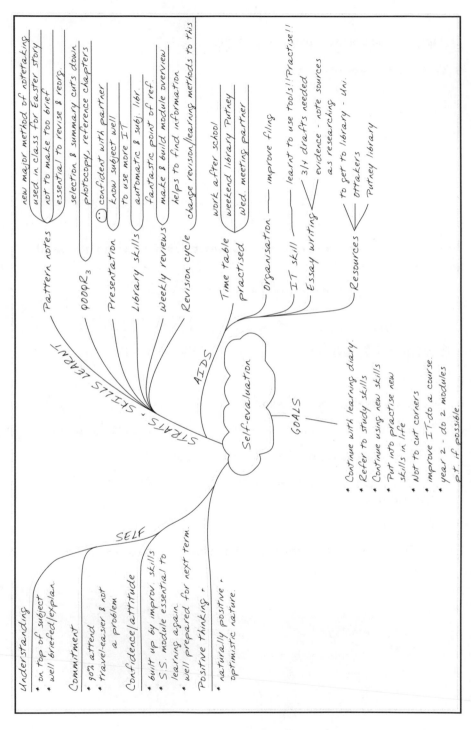

Figure 10.3 A self-assessment of a study skills programme

Conclusion

In this section we prompted you to complete a detailed self-assessment with respect to your use of the various study and academic skills and practices that we have covered in the book as a whole (see Fig 10.3 for a sample self-assessment). How do you feel now? What will you do next?

By now you should be feeling ready to tackle anything that college or university can throw at you – and we just want to wish you luck. If you do still have any remaining issues:

- Why not go to see the Learning Development or Support Unit at your institution?
- Why not go and see the Student Support Services people?
- Sort things out with your study partner?

Remembering to use essential study and academic skills and practices

We stress that all the activities covered in this text will help you to succeed in your studies, and they will work to increase your enjoyment of and confidence in the academic environment – but will you remember them?

We have devised a mnemonic to help you remember the six steps to success (see the Introduction). To do this we summarised the six steps, took the first letter from each section and got the acronym SOCCER. Remember SOCCER to ensure your study success!

- **S – Study techniques and practices:** organise yourself for study – use all the resources of your university – become familiar with academic practice – remember your QOOQRRR, your SQP4, and the 'how to…' of group work, assignments etc.

- **O – Overview:** use your course handbooks – read the aims and learning outcomes – use these to direct your revision and exam strategies.

- **C – Creativity:** brainstorm and question matrix ideas – practise your pattern notes.

- **C – Communicate effectively:** using the academic conventions and practices of your subject – see Chapter 9 – how to prepare better assignments.

- **E – Emotions – build your motivation:** use the learning contract. Deal with your fear – build your self-confidence – see Chapter 7 – how to build your confidence.

- **R – Review, review, review:** use the revision cycle and the reflective learning diary. Use it or lose it. Review your learning – and your learning strategies.

INDEX